THEORIES OF DEMOCRATIC GOVERNANCE
IN THE INSTITUTIONS OF HIGHER EDUCATION

A WALDEN UNIVERSITY'S UNIT OF STUDY: BREADTH COMPONENT OF THE ADVANCED KNOWLEDGE AREA MODULE NUMBER V

THEORIES OF DEMOCRATIC GOVERNANCE IN THE INSTITUTIONS OF HIGHER EDUCATION

Emmanuel N. A. Tetteh, M.S., B.P.S.

Ph.D. Student in Public Policy and Administration
School of Management
Walden University

[handwritten inscription and signature]

iUniverse, Inc.
New York Lincoln Shanghai

Theories of Democratic Governance
in the Institutions of Higher Education

iUniverse, Inc.

For information address:
iUniverse, Inc.
2021 Pine Lake Road, Suite 100
Lincoln, NE 68512
www.iuniverse.com

ISBN: 0-595-31465-1 (pbk)
ISBN: 0-595-76890-3 (cloth)

Printed in the United States of America

I dedicate this research document of the Advanced Knowledge Area Module Number V to service-learners and civic administrators whose vision and dedication to civic responsibility serve as the ideal for the democratization of institutions of higher education in human society.

ACKNOWLEDGMENTS

First and foremost, I would like to thank my God Almighty for His grace that has enabled me to move this expository research project forward. I am also thankful for Walden University's unique Knowledge Area Module (KAM) demonstration, without which it would not have been possible for me to write this research document.

More importantly, I would like to thank Dr. Karen Treiber (my Faculty Mentor/KAM Assessor & Chair of my Dissertation Supervisory Committee) for her profound guidance, encouragement, academic support, constructive criticism, scrutiny in producing a scholarly work, and her willingness to challenge me to utilize my writing skills effectively in documenting this KAM demonstration. I also thank Dr. Gary Keseley, who served as the second assessor of this KAM project. For this, I am grateful to Dr. Marion Angelica, the Chair of the Public Policy and Administration Program in the School of Management, for nominating these profound Walden faculty members to work with in this Breadth component of the Advanced Knowledge Area Module Number V.

Finally, I want to acknowledge the support of my spouse, Regina Tetteh, for her moral support, understanding, and encouragement that helped me to concentrate on writing and typing this document. Above all, I am thankful to the publishing companies for the permissions granted, without which it would not have been possible to publish this derivative research manuscript. In fact, it is their books that served as the main resources for this KAM research project. They include: HarperCollins Publishers (formerly Harper & Brothers), McGraw-Hill Book Company, Brookings Institution, Macmillan Company (An imprint of Simon & Schuster Adult Publishing Group), Palgrave Macmillan, Lynne Rienner Publishers, The Kettering Foundation, and Peter Lang Publishing Company. To them, I am greatly indebted.

CONTENTS

List of Tables and Figures

PREFACE

This book is one of my research projects in the doctoral program in Public Policy and Administration in the School of Management at Walden University. It is a slightly expanded version of the one submitted to the Walden Institution, which served as one of the ground works toward my doctoral dissertation research project. Increased concern about societal security and interest into how human institutions can contribute to the civility of society makes this book not only unique, but also a current issue in the exploration of the tenets of democratic governance. Since the United States exemplifies an idyllic system of democratic governance, one is led to think that every aspect of its institution may be committed to civic ideals. Unfortunately, until recent years, many American institutions of higher education are perceived as having displaced the core goal of their civic missions. But should not the civic missions of higher education focus instead on the training of the mind? Or is there any moral obligation for the institutions of higher education to direct their civic missions toward societal civility or democratic governance? This book attempts to provide answers to these crucial issues.

While the appearance of higher education's non-involvement in democratic governance of civic society may be troubling, some nations, especially in the Third World, have had difficulty even experimenting with the ideals of democracy. Other nations like Ghana, for example, have had unsteady system of democratic rule. Since the aftermath of the initial *coup d'état* in 1966 that interrupted the First Democratic Republic of Ghana, the Ghanaian people suffered several setbacks in democratic governance. Inevitable, the quest for a representative form of government became an outburst cry for most Ghanaians, and for which the Ghanaian institutions of higher education and the Ghana Bar Association played critical role in returning Ghana to democratic rule. The history of the democratic actions of higher education, however, can be traced back to the medieval universities, so what went wrong and caused the decline in civic engagement of higher education administration? By addressing this concern, the book attempts to provide some insight into the democratic culture of higher education in the United States and Ghana.

The book represents the *Breadth*[1] component of the *Knowledge Area Module*[2] (KAM) V, which investigated essential contemporary democratic issues in higher education administration from their theoretical and historical contexts. In accomplishing this, I examined the role of higher education that influences public policy and guides the administrative decision-making process to foster civility. In this context, the theories of democratic governance and public policy were analyzed as they relate to the administrative practices of enrollment management in institutions of higher education and their underlying assumptions on open access to adult education and civic/democratic education. As a contextual framework, this research document focused on three critical premises—*analysis, synthesis,* and *evaluation*—in examining five potential *Breadth Theories*[3], including three other resources that helped explore the applicability of these theories from the contemporary and historical democratic perspectives.

My experiences and research interests in several areas in higher education administrative services, as well as my work as adjunct faculty at the Metropolitan College of New York (MCNY), provided the framework that led me into this derivative research. These research interests include enrollment management, service-learning, experiential education, democratic education, and civic responsibility of institutions of higher education. With the commitment to scholarly research and contribution to the body of knowledge, I graduated with the highest distinction in both the Baccalaureate and Master's Degree programs. Upon the completion of my Master's Degree action research project at MCNY, I discovered, formulated and elaborated a metaphorical concept that I called *Communal Photosynthesis*[SM]. This theory is contained in my 324-page copyrighted Master's thesis entitled *An Agency for Recruitment Affairs: Using Functional-Context-Training Program and Marketing Management Techniques to Improve Enrollment Management*. While building on this theory is the focal point of my dissertation research project, the redacted version of this Master's thesis manuscript is also under consideration for publication.

In addition, my public service experience includes approximately 18 years of ministerial work, which has contributed to societal values, maximization of human potential, and civic ideals of the American community, as well as the communities of other nationals. Specifically, my contributions to church ministry include counseling people with growing psychosocial problems from all walks of life, writing two Biblical studies, and teaching at church conferences and seminars: 1) *The Importance of Christian Fellowship* in 1995; and 2) *The Principles of Obtaining the Exaltation of God* in 1996. These experiences helped shape my knowledge base in the democratic moral values and civic causes of our society and provided a formidable perspective into the writing of this book. In the following three chapters, I shall examine the contents of civic involvement, democratic action, civic education, and democratic governance in the practices of higher education administration.

---

[1]Represents one of the Walden University's Knowledge Area Module criteria for which students demonstrates higher level of critical analysis and integration of theoretical knowledge (Walden University Catalog 2003-2004).

[2]A Walden University's unit of study in a specific subject area, which allows students to conduct an independent investigation based on an approved Learning Agreement (LA) by faculty mentor(s) who serves as the KAM demonstration assessor(s) for which students demonstrate the Breadth, Depth and Application of a body of knowledge that addresses real-world challenges (Walden University Catalog 2003-2004).

[3]A derivative research projects of five potential theories of democratic governance—works by Harold Raymond Wayne Benjamin and Associates, David Breneman and Chester Finn, John Dewey, Robert Pinkney, and the editorial work of Bernard Murchland, and three additional resources—Constance Ewing Cook, the editorial work of Steven Schapiro, and the 1947 Report of the President's Commission on Higher Education that helped explored the applicability of the theories from an historical and a contemporary democratic perspective.

INTRODUCTION

In what ways can higher education live up to its civic missions? Should the security of society be of any concern to higher education, and in what ways can colleges and universities contribution to societal civility? Realizing the uncertainty in human society regarding an existence of a responsive democratic action for institutions of higher education in societal governance, in this research manuscript, the author explores important theoretical and historical democratic paradigms. While there is growing skepticism concerning the role of higher education in democratic systems of governance, such cynicism does not preclude the fact that the civic missions of colleges and universities are integral for effective facilitation of societal civility. It is possible that because higher education is more concerned with "the development of the mind, of the capacity to reason," it is recognized as "the best guarantor of any kind of competence—civic or otherwise" to the extent that "questions about how a political community should act, was pushed outside the walls of academe" (Mathews in Murchland, 1991, pp. 48–49).

Following these concerns, this Breadth component of the Knowledge Area Module (KAM) Number V will investigate the theories of democratic governance and public policy as they relate to the administrative practices and underlying assumptions of open access to adult and civic educations. According to the Report of the President's Commission on Higher Education (1947), "It is a commonplace of the democratic faith that education is indispensable to the maintenance and growth of freedom of thought, faith, enterprise, and association" (p. 5, Vol. 1). Underscoring the premise of these notions, this Knowledge Area Module will concentrate on the analysis, synthesis, and evaluation of five theories of democratic governance, hereafter referred to as the "*Breadth Theories*," except when they are examined on an individual basis.

The five theories explored here include works by Harold Raymond Wayne Benjamin and Associates, David Breneman and Chester Finn,

John Dewey, Robert Pinkney, and the editorial work of Bernard Murchland. By way of examining these Breadth Theories in terms of contemporary public policy issues and democratic practices of higher education, the theoretical research project of Constance Ewing Cook and the editorial work of Steven Schapiro will be relevantly applied. In addition, as a means of exploring the applicability of these theories from an historical and a contemporary democratic perspective as they relate to higher education, the researcher will analyze a twentieth century evaluation of the 1947 Report of the President's Commission on Higher Education.

Throughout history, people have formed governments either as constitutional monarchies or as republics. While some forms of government may be unacceptable or remain questionable, some nations have their systems of rule formed by *coups d'état* and totalitarian regimes. Underlying these systems of government is the core objective of a functional structure that keeps up with the rule of law, preserves civic order, protects property rights, promotes inalienable rights, fosters the pursuit of happiness, and maintains security against aggression or foreign invasion (Baradat, 2003). The ideal form of the functional government that aspires to these fundamental human rights, liberties, and the rules of law reflect the preamble of the Constitution of the United States of America (Corwin, 1920; Wilson, 2000). This functional structure of government is exemplified by a political system that gives mandate on how laws, beliefs, ideals, regulations, and policies should be executed for the betterment of the society for which it exists and operates (Ball and Dagger, 2002; Pinkney, 1994; & Wilson, 2000). Thus, it follows that in the absence of government, there is a feeling of anarchy that makes people fear that society is doomed toward danger (Baradat, 2003; & Pinkney, 1994), so inhabitants of all nations oblige themselves to submit to the ideals that foster societal governance.

Just as there is diversity among opinions within the populace, so too, the political system of government reflects several political ideologies or persuasions to which government aspires in order to maintain reasonable civility. Paramount among these political ideologies is the

Aristotelian classification of governments structured to maximize the interest of the public and/or the self. Those serving the public interest are categorized as monarchy, aristocracy, and polity, while those meant for self-interest are noted as tyranny, oligarchy, and democracy (Ball & Dagger, 2002). To a certain extent, some levels of skepticism exist among society as to which of these realms of persuasions is most appealing. However, "with respect to political ideologies, it is felt that democracy is an ideal that most ideologies espouse; but because people have very different understandings of what democracy is, they pursue it in very different ways" (Ball & Dagger, 2002, p. 20).

According to Shafritz and Russell (2000), "The term democracy often has been used by totalitarian regimes and their *people's democracies*; one person's democratic regime is too often another's totalitarian despotism; so modern democracy, like the modern contact lens, is in the eye of the beholder" (p. 44). Arguably, some political philosophers contend that not every democracy should be perceived as the most ideal form of societal governance since it can be hijacked into tyranny by malfeasance or a totalitarian regime. One possible explanation for this is that some followers of different ideologies simply have their own ideas regarding the ways to achieve democracy, and as such, they use it in hypocritical or deceptive way (Ball & Dagger, 2002). Agreeably, Shafritz and Russell (2000) point out that "Aristotle had warned in several instances about the so-called 'pure' democracy of ancient Athens that they had often been captured by demagogues and degenerated into dictatorial tyrannies" (p. 45). More so, given the strengths and weaknesses inherent in democratic governance, coupled with the cynicisms that surround the different political persuasions about which form of government will better serve the common good of the citizenry, democracy in all shapes and forms has its own flaws (Ball & Dagger, 2002).

Underpinning these viewpoints, in his ironic statement of the 1814 letter, John Adams wrote: "Remember, democracy never lasts long. It soon wastes, exhausts, and murders itself. There never was a democracy yet that did not commit suicide" (in Shafritz & Russell, 2000, p. 45). In 1947, while coming to grips with the growing skepticism of an ideal democracy, Winston Churchill declared to the House of Commons, "No one pretends that democracy is perfect or all wise. Indeed, it has been said that democracy is the worst form of government except all those other forms that have been tried from time to time" (in Shafritz & Russell, 2000, p. 45).

While John Adams's assertion that democracy is suicidal suggests its imperfections, it must be noted that the longevity of democratic governance has, for the most part, contributed to civility within the human community. Also, some suggest it is indeed the consummate form of government (Ball & Dagger, 2002). Not only is the pursuit of democratic governance seen as an idyllic venture of great benefit to societal stability and respect for the rule of law, it also serves as the mechanism for maximizing the political economy and socialization of a nation (Pinkney, 1994).

Integral to the goals of democracy is the premise that the citizenry must be taught the skills necessary for living in a democratic society. Included in these essential skills are the abilities to communicate effectively, to read and write, to internalize basic values and beliefs, and to develop a sense of responsibility or responsible citizenship. Fulfilling these civic responsibilities requires the substantial participation of families, educational institutions, religious bodies, economics institutions, and local and national government entities (Cohen & Orbuch, 1990; Benjamin & Associates, 1950; Dewey, 1916, 1938; Hickey, Voorhees & Associates, 1969; Murchland, 1991; Skocpol & Fiorina, 1999). On this note, the Center for Democracy and Governance (1998) contends, "The hallmark of democratic society is the freedom of individuals to associate with like-minded individuals, express their views publicly, openly debate public policy and petition their government" (p. 15).

Since there appear to be opposing viewpoints on the ideology of democratic governance, it is most prudent that these Breadth Theories be critically examined in order to produce a comprehensive stance. Therefore, for the purpose of ascertaining the ways in which these democratic theories relate to institutions of higher education, what follows are the critical analysis, synthesis, and evaluation of the Breadth Theories.

PART 1

ANALYSIS OF THE BREADTH THEORIES IN DEMOCRATIC ACTIONS OF HIGHER EDUCATION

CHAPTER 1

EXPOSITION OF DEMOCRATIC IDEALS OF THE BREADTH THEORIES

Harold Raymond Wayne Benjamin and Associates

a) <u>*The Role of Higher Education in National Development*</u>:

In his 1965 work on *Higher Education in the American Republics*, Harold Raymond Wayne Benjamin hypothesized that the quality of higher education and its benefit to a democratic society is connected to the degree of national development. Thus, as institutions of higher education fail to meet their democratic responsibilities, so, too, will the social and cultural infrastructures of their homeland decline to the extent that they become hostile to the democratization of the society. Institutions of higher education are the social and intellectual fabrics of a nation (Benjamin, 1950), designed "as an instrument of advanced communication and social progress. It cannot operate in a cultural vacuum. It is designed to serve a particular culture. Its basis is that culture's past. Its orientation is the improvement of that culture's future" (Benjamin, 1965, p. 3). Benjamin infers that the primary democratic ideal of institutions of higher education is to promote the progressive strength of the cultural values of a nation. This progressive strength for which institutions of higher learning exist to advance toward community development "depends solely upon the way in which each individual in this community of interested people will put his [or her] own strength at the service of the ideal" (Taylor in Benjamin, 1950, pp. 41–42).

From Benjamin's standpoint, the ideal cultural values of a democratic nation epitomize the social fabric and democratic association of the community for which the people live in pursuit and advancement of *higher values*. Benjamin acknowledged these higher values as involving the training of the minds of people for higher capacity and higher truth, and fitting them for higher callings in which there is a cultivation of the intellect toward character development. Therefore the mission of higher education should focus on transforming those areas of human life associated with higher values, which can be obtained by engaging the learning energies of the citizenry toward a democratic ideal. However, Hullfish (1950) noted, "The valuing men do is conditioned by the quality of the human associations within which the valuing is done" (p. 49). So then, the creation of an ideal democratic relationship is perhaps possible in the context of a learning association that promotes moral efficacy of shared democratic experience. Characterized by civic virtues, this democratic ideal is to build an institution in which every participant is committed to sharing the common aims of the democratic association. The ideal democratic association is a dynamic interactive process involving the ends-means procedures employed by a group of people for the goal of solving a common problem of democratic society (Benjamin, 1950 & 1965). So crucial should be an institutional concern of solving the civic problem of the human community since the existence of *lower values* can threaten the ideals of democratic society. Connecting with this institutional democratic ideal, Benjamin (1950) avowed:

> A democracy is a manner of association whereby men order their own ways for their own benefit. A democratic education is that phase of their association whereby they change their own ways in the direction of their own ideals. The purpose of higher education in a democracy can therefore be discovered only by observing the democracy in action. (p. 4)

b) <u>*Comparison of the Historical & Contemporary Contexts of Higher Education Democracy*</u>:

From the historical perspective, Benjamin (1950 & 1965) observed that democracy in action has shown that the medieval university, for instance, bore a relatively slight resemblance to modern institutions of higher education. This is based on the perception that the medieval university had no great concern with tangential matters, but instead of those crucial to democratic ideals and values. As a case in point, between the thirteenth and fourteenth centuries, the medieval university was perceived as a democratic institution at the time when church and state eluded the notion that anyone other than the pope, the emperor, the king, the bishop, or any other divinely appointed superior should decide what was best for the people to do and think.

In the intervening time, the evolution of the medieval institutions of higher education, officially known as *stadium generale,* dated back to the twelfth century and had only five European universities: Salerno and Bologna in Italy, Montpellier and Paris in France, and Oxford in England. Benjamin (1965), however, noted that all modern universities can be traced to the twelfth-century *universitas* of Paris and Bologna. Originally, the term *universitas* (meaning the whole, the entire group or corporation) did not refer to the institution, but to the organization of people who operated the *stadium generale.* For example, in Paris, the *universitas* was the corporation of masters, while in Bologna it was the corporation of students. Although, the concept of university organization and administration in the United States exemplifies the *universitas* of Paris, it was superseded in matters of general policy by lay boards of trustees or regents representing each university's constituency (Benjamin, 1950).

The aims of the institutions of higher education in colonial Spanish America during the sixteenth through the eighteenth centuries focused on the training of members of the liberal professions, namely theology, law, medicine, and the arts. However, the most dynamic democratic action group in the institutions of higher education in the first half of the eighteenth century was the Society of Jesus, whose primary aim was to train clerical and lay leaders in the furtherance of religious and political endeavors of the Society. By and large, these colonial universities of Spanish America were founded, administered, controlled, and supported by church authorities, and for those institutions under a specific religious order, by that order's leaders. While the University of Costa Rica was established in 1843 by liberal and democratic groups, it held onto the old colonial tradition in its organization and methods during most of the nineteenth century (Benjamin, 1965).

Before the American Revolution, there were only nine colleges in colonial America: Harvard in Massachusetts (1636), which in 1780 the Massachusetts' constitution referred to as the University at Cambridge, William and Mary in Virginia (1693), Yale in Connecticut (1701), which became Yale University in 1887, the College of New Jersey (1746), which became Princeton University in 1896, King's College in New York (1754), which became Columbia University in 1924, the College and Academy at Philadelphia (1755), which was the first to change its name to the University of Philadelphia in 1791, the College of Rhode Island (1764), which became Brown University in 1804, Queen's College in New Jersey (1766), which changed its name to Rutgers University in 1924, and Dartmouth in New Hampshire (1769). Apart from the College of Philadelphia, which later fell under the influence of the Episcopalians, these colonial colleges were founded under Protestant religious auspices (Benjamin, 1965).

In the second decade of the twentieth century, a university reform movement arose in Spanish America that led to a more democratic administration in colonial institutions of higher learning. However, the underlying aim of these colonial universities, "was the transmittal of higher culture which was regarded as a unitary body of attitudes and knowledge coming down through proper Calvinist and other Protestant sources" (Benjamin, 1965, p. 36).

From the contemporary point of view, while higher education has held on to democratic ideals, it is also perceived as having displaced the values of democratic actions. These democratic actions, which include civic engagement, political participation, and moral education for citizenship, declined until the mid 1980s when the call for renewal of institutions of higher education as agents of democracy stirred up an interest in service-learning programs at many schools. For instance, data from an annual survey of college freshmen indicated that participation in political affairs or activities had dropped from a high of 30 percent in 1968 down to 15 percent in 1995 (Ehrlich, 2000; Jacoby & Associates,1996). Again, Jacoby and Associates (1996) noted that "The service-learning movement that had acquired a foothold on college campuses in the 1960s and 1970s did not last" (p.13). For this, a great concern arose among advocates for civic engagement as to the imminent threat that this abandonment in the service-learning movement could have on the democratic actions of the institutions of higher education. These advocates believe that there is a clear-cut link between democratic action and service-learning responsibility of higher education, and for which revitalization is imperative (Ehrlich, 2000; Eyler & Giles, 1999; Etzioni, 1993; Jacoby & Associates, 1996; Putnam, 2000; Skocpol & Fiorina, 1999).

c) *Correlation of Democratic Action and Social Responsibility of Higher Education in Higher Culture Development*:

By showing some degree of correlation between democratic action and higher educational responsibility in higher culture development, Hand (1950) also posited that, "By virtue of the central value it strives to embody, a democratic society places a heavy responsibility upon its institutions of higher learning in reference to the diagnosis of students" (p. 165). This diagnosis entails studying the institutions' students and their communities in terms of relevant democratic values and concerns of modern society (Benjamin, 1950 & 1965), "since our institutions of higher learning, in concert with the lower schools, are supposed to be laboratories of democracy in which the democratic way of life is learned through living democratically as well as through formal instruction" (Hand in Benjamin, 1950, p. 80).

Addressing these relevant democratic values and concerns of higher culture development in modern society, the President's Commission on

Higher Education (1947) observed, "The social role of education in a democratic society is at once to insure equal liberty and equal opportunity to differing individuals and groups, and to enable the citizens to understand, appraise, and redirect forces, men, and events as these tend to strengthen or weaken their liberties" (p. 5, Vol. 1). The commission, however, contended that, "In performing this role, education will necessarily vary its means and methods to fit the diversity of its constituency, but it will achieve its ends more successfully if its programs and polices grow out of and are relevant to the characteristics and needs of contemporary society" (pp. 5–6). It thus implies that the commission recognized the cause of the role of higher education in higher culture development as a variable that can affect social change in democratic life. On this basis, the commission concurred that, "The discovery, training, and utilization of individual talents is of fundamental importance in a free society. To liberate and perfect the intrinsic powers of every citizen is the central purpose of democracy, and its furtherance of individual self-realization is its greatest glory" (p. 9). Furthermore, the commission postulated that, "An educational system finds its guiding principles and ultimate goals in the aims and philosophy of the social order in which it functions. The two predominant types of society in the world today are democratic and the authoritarian, and the social role of education is very different in the two systems" (p. 5, Vol. 1).

To a greater degree, Benjamin's 1950 and 1965 works account that there were shifts in the social order toward democratic ideals, shaping the aims of the institutions of higher education. The transmission of this higher culture most specifically called for the development of a *democratic dynamic* in the cultural context of the human society. Referring to this democratic dynamic, the President's Commission on Higher Education argued, "It is imperative that American education develop a democratic dynamic that will inspire faith in the democratic way of life, dispel doubt and defeatism about the future, and imbue youth with the conviction that life has high purpose and that they are active and responsible participants in the purpose" (President's Commission on Higher Education, 1947, p. 102, Vol. 1).

In addition, Taylor (in Benjamin, 1950) stressed that, "the total aim of higher education is to induce certain attitudes and values, principal among which is the valuing of knowledge as personally significant and socially useful" (p. 33). Confirming these aims, the Report of the President's Commission on Higher Education, declared, "The first goal in education for democracy is the full rounded, and continuing development of the person…The fundamental concept of democracy is a belief in the inherent worth of the individual, in the dignity and value of human life" (pp. 9 & 11, Vol. 1). Therefore, from Benjamin's stance, this higher culture for democratic living is comprised of attitudes, values, and knowledge for personal and social development.

By drawing a parallel between the higher culture for democratic living and individual and social development, in Benjamin (1950), Hornbake argued that, "since in a democracy, the ultimate purpose of education is the optimum growth of the individual, the neglect of social purpose and the neglect of individuality are two ways of saying the same thing" (p. 183). Hence, Benjamin's position tends to affirm the anticipated causal relationship between the intervening variables— *values* and *knowledge*—and the concept of *higher culture* shaped by democratic education. So then, Benjamin's presumed cause and effect relationships established here seem to denote the individual and social responsibilities of democratic living that uphold the higher culture of national development.

d) *Causality of Democratic Education in Societal Security Management and Communal Responsibility*:

In undergirding the individual and social responsibilities of democratic living in relationship to the role of higher education toward higher culture and national development, Benjamin (1950) posited, "The democracy of the earliest universities arose in response to a need for *security* in study" (p. 7). While not explicitly stated, Benjamin's assertion points to the analogy that just as the United States was founded as a result of the pilgrims fleeing religious persecution, the colonial universities evolved in the quest for human inquiry into societal security management. Hence, Benjamin's hypothesis is that the democratic responsibility of the colonial universities stemmed from an overwhelming need for research into security concerns of the national culture served by those institutions of higher learning. In pointing out that the democratic research needs of the colonial universities were responsive to their security challenges, Benjamin's supposition adds weight to Hornbake's assertion that, "Higher education should select its activities not on the basis of *privileged learning* for *privileged persons* but rather upon the contribution which education can make towards solving a problem of social consequence" (Hornbake in Benjamin, 1950, p. 194).

More so, what echoed the democratic readiness of higher education's research interest in mitigating social concerns is the argument that higher education research should focus on those problems that are pressing upon the society, including those insignificant ills that may soon become acute. The degree of research interest should not only focus on domestic, local, or labor group problems, but also continue to the extent that its contribution can develop international understandings in matters so pressing to the human community (Hornbake in Benjamin, 1950). This argues the President's Commission on Higher Education (1947) assertion that, "Effective democratic education will deal directly with current problems" (p. 6) Attesting to the democratic research interests that addressed the problems of social consequences, Benjamin (1965) claimed that the colonial universities focused their studies on the quest for answers to three primary research questions/problems: "1) How secure are the people, and/or what is the state of their health, safety, personal rights, and social welfare? 2) How productive are the people? 3) How cultivated are the people?" (Benjamin, 1965, pp. 3–4).

Underpinning these colonial universities' research interests, in Benjamin (1950), Johnson stressed "…our academic institutions are a part of the community and should expect to give spark and direction to its life. The issues which are live, vital issues in the society should be those on which education is concentrating its resources and its techniques; and what is taught in school should be taught in relation to its function as a part of the social fabric" (p. 21). Also, since, Hullfish (1950) professed that, "the essence of higher education and, indeed, of democracy, is found in the pooling of different ideas for the purpose of seeking better ones," the role of higher education in promoting scientific research in security concerns can establish a measure of reliability for societal security management. For instance, Benjamin (1950) claimed that, by and large, the lecturers at the University of Paris were foreigners and thus had limited rights, so they formed a democratic association for mutual protection. Likewise, at the University of Bologna, the international students felt an enormous need for protection while studying, and their only sense of safety came from the establishment of a democratic alliance.

Equally significant, to underscore the notion of the higher culture that sets the parameters for democratic action within institutions of higher education, Benjamin (1965) affirmed, "The crucial measure of a university's distinction is how well it does in developing programs to improve the people's *security, productivity,* and *cultivation* within the limits set by its culture" (p. 4). In using the statistical denotation *crucial measure,* Benjamin was not only suggesting that the causal relationship that may exist between higher education's programs and the citizen's security, productivity, and cultivation toward higher culture development can be measured, but it may also explain the terms contained in his hypothesis. The underlying premise of higher education's programs suggested by Benjamin is *democratic education,* since, as previously noted, he acknowledged that democracy is a matter of association, and democratic education is the context of that association. By strengthening these lines of argument, Benjamin (1950) theorized that:

> Democracy is only an instrument to get things done for a people. It is only a tool for utilizing the maximum intelligence of a group. The university needs democracy not because democracy is a sacred word but because the university has to get something

done for its people. If it does not get done what the people need to have done, the people will once again ride by the university as they rode by its medieval predecessor. If the modern American university finally demonstrates that it received from its academic ancestors too many costumes and ceremonials and not enough principles and springs of action it too can end up staring in scholarly solemnity at its institutional navel. (p. 14)

Most importantly, what needs to be underscored here is that Benjamin is, in fact, correlating the effects of security, productivity, and cultivation as interdependent variables for which the cause of the ideal democratic education induces the progressive strength for higher culture and national development. For this correlation, Benjamin (1965) undeniably averred that, "These three areas of national endeavor—security, productivity, and cultivation—are interdependent" (p. 4). As interdependent variables, they seem to contain "internal consistency" (Mark, 1996; O'Sullivan, Rassel, & Berner, 2003; Singleton & Straits, 1988) since all three areas of these national endeavors constitute measures relating to the same phenomenon of higher democratic culture development. Substantiating this viewpoint, Benjamin (1965) argued that, "To achieve security, people have to be productive and cultivated. Increase of one's productivity requires both cultivation and security. Finally, cultivation results when freedom is exercised in a productive environment" (p. 4). Also, attributable to this internal consistency in Benjamin's supposition on the cultivation of freedom, the President's Commission moreover affirmed that, "individual freedom entails *communal responsibility*. The democratic way of life can endure only as private careers and social obligation are made to mesh, as personal ambition is reconciled with public responsibility" (The Report of the President's Commission on Higher Education, 1947, p. 10, Vol. 1).

Endemic to this communal responsibility, Hand (in Benjamin 1950) suggested that institutions of higher education must establish a research framework for outlining community study that can promote certain basic *social processes* to advance good societal health. However, to maximize the progressive strength of these social processes, these institutions must demand learned behavior and social responsibility that can be acquired through democratic education. Included in the array of the social processes on which the community study should be focused are vocational education, data on world cultures, health data, natural resources data, child rearing data, esthetic and spiritual data, leisure time data, values data, and government data. While these social processes of community study are vital to higher culture and national developments, the data on world cultures, natural resources, and governing seem to be the most crucial areas for research studies. For instance, regarding the data on world cultures, Hand contended that every society is obligated to provide sound physical and internal security for its citizenry in an effort to ensure world peace. Most community studies on the culture of security concerns, however, have been severely restricted to a certain few Western nations, thus the cultures of Asia, Africa, and South America must still be studied.

e) <u>*Democratic Administration in Higher Education and Open Access Policy*</u>:

Finally, Benjamin and Associates (1950) pointed out that another aspect of the progressive strength of institutions of higher education lies in the specialization of administrators and the intellectual body. The function of this specialization must foster democratic administration that provides a mechanism for intercommunication among individuals, departments, and the college community. In addition, it must uphold sensitivity to the principle of participative democracy within which each person shares responsibility in the decision-making process and/or policy formation that guides the educational process toward democratic living. However, since every society has a its own unique goal toward higher culture development, higher education administration must develop a policy coalition that aids access to college education and promotes its unique responsibility in democratic education. Adding to these policy issues, according to Cook (1998):

Higher education, like every policy community has a special culture and self-image that shape its federal relations structure and lobbying strategies in unique ways. The higher education community puts a particular high priority on consensus building. That priority is evident in the well-defined association structure that overlays and integrates the community through a system of overlapping memberships across network. (p. 117)

In addressing how these policy issues impact the enrollment management of higher education in terms of federal financial aid on open access, the author will now analyze the tenets of Breneman and Finn (1978).

This expository research is based on selected excerpts from *Democracy in the Administration of Higher Education,* edited by Harold R. W. Benjamin, Tenth Yearbook of the John Dewey Society. Copyright, 1950, by Harper & Brothers. Reprinted with permission of HarperCollins Publishers Inc. The analysis is also based on selected excerpts from *Higher Education in the American Republics,* by Harold R. W. Benjamin, Copyright © 1965 by McGraw-Hill Book Company. Reprinted with permission of the publisher.

David Breneman and Chester Finn

i) *Public Policy and Enrollment Management Malaises in Higher Education*:

Despite the rising trend of growth in private higher education in the mid 1970s, Breneman and Finn, in their 1978 studies and editorial work on *Public Policy and Private Higher Education*, recognized the need for examining the opposing forces that have the potential to affect public policy at the state and federal levels, and thus impact upon institutional policymakers. Breneman and Finn were, for the most part, concerned about the rising cost of higher education, escalating failure in economic returns to college graduates, demographic trends contributing to enrollment malaises in higher education, revenue competitiveness, and the need for public policy proposals to shape institutional vitality. Of particular note is a study of the eighteen-year-old age group in the U.S. population for the years 1970 through 1993, which portrayed a record increase of 4.3 million freshmen matriculation in 1979, but declined drastically to a low of 3.2 million in 1992. They noted, however, that enrollment in private institutions of higher education doubled from 1950 to 1976, increasing from 1.14 million to 2.39 million, but in the public institutions, the enrollment figures increased from 1.15 million to 7.44 million. By and large, two-year colleges accounted for most of this enrollment growth, increasing from 218,000 degree-credit students in 1950 to an estimated 2.65 million in 1976.

ii) *Disparity of Open Access to Higher Education*:

In respect to the opposing forces, Breneman and Finn (1978) observed that there is inequality in the geographic distribution of private institutions of higher learning within the United States. They contend that this can be best explained in terms of the broad disparity that exists in the pedagogical role of the private sector's higher education communities in each state, thus creating differences in policies between the public and private institutions of higher learning. The variation reflects the types of controls exercised by each state's government as they have different systems of interacting with their own institutions of higher education.

Most disturbingly, however, the extent of the disparity in the geographic distribution of open access to higher education sets hurdles in the context that attempts to link the federal and state policies to a levelheaded and mutually beneficial pattern. This resonates with the concern of the President's Commission on Higher Education (1947) that, "the barriers mean that far too few of our young people are getting enough preparation for assuming the personal, social, and civic responsibilities of adults living in a democratic society" (p. 35, Vol. 1). More so, what seems to complicate this disparity is a significant difference in the proportion of matriculated students from out-of-state and of those from the local market niche of the private institutions of higher learning. Also, in the early 1970s, the tuition gap showed a decline in the financial value of a college education due to the decreasing rates in the matriculation of white males, as well as a demographic decline in the traditional college-going age groups (Breneman & Finn, 1978; Cook, 1998). Thus, the need to study the variables that serve as the determinants of the demand for higher education, which includes tuition costs and income effects, labor market effects, financial aid influence, alterations in institutional behavior, curricula effects, and enrollment policy effects, becomes apparent.

Breneman and Finn suggest that while in principle public and private colleges have equal access to federal programs, it does not guarantee equal treatment because of their distinctive features, and so they are affected by federal policies in quite different ways. For instance, in the academic year 1973-74, the federal direct payments to colleges and universities amounted to $4.46 billion; however, just about 39.2 percent went to private institutions compared to 60.8 percent that went to public ones. Moreover, Breneman and Finn postulate that one distinct feature of the free enterprise system in higher education shows that not every venture may be successful since the potential for failure is unpredictably associated with independence and innovation. Strikingly, Cook (1998) noted that "in spite of the significance of the higher education enterprise, there is no comprehensive federal policy regarding

colleges and universities. Federal involvement in higher education policy making has always been piecemeal, and role of the national government is ambiguous" (p. 5).

iii) *Causality of Federal Student Aid Policy on Open Access into Higher Education*:

On the policy question as to whether the three largest federal student
aid programs (the GI bill, student stipends paid through the social security system, and the educational opportunity grants) are equally service-
able to students at both private and public colleges and universities,
Breneman and Finn hypothesized that it, "depends on the *fit* [italics
added] between the costs of attending particular colleges and the levels
of assistance provided by particular federal programs" (Breneman &
Finn, 1978, p. 35). Here, the *fit* concept, as used by Breneman and Finn,
tends to depict an *association variable* in the sense that the hypothesis
contains a cause and effect relationship that may be statistically associated. More so, the causality of Breneman and Finn's hypothesis as stated
may be posited as representing a *continuous statement* since the increases
in the costs of attending specific colleges are associated with the increases
in the levels of assistance provided by specific federal programs.

In this case, the independent variable (the costs of attending specific
colleges) may include tuition impact, income viability, private *versus* public higher education choice for matriculation, and state and institutional
enrollment policy. Also, the dependent variable (the levels of assistance
provided by particular federal programs) may involve the students' financial aid programs, federal policies, community interest, and public policy
influence. Furthermore, in this editorial work, McPherson (1978)
attempted to establish the connection of this *fit* concept in terms of the
interplay that shapes enrollment demand in higher education. The
McPherson viewpoint tends to affirm that access to higher education is
mostly affected by the tuition factor and the federal programs that can
alleviate the tuition roadblock. For this, the President's Commission on
Higher Education (1947) observed that open access to higher education is

democracy's obligation and a necessity for citizens' social development, since "education is the foundation of democratic liberties" (p. 25, Vol. 1).

Given the magnitude of the interplay between federal programs and enrollment demands in higher education, if "student subsidies" are not favored by an equitable policy to open access "the trade-off between access and choice will continue"…to the extent that "fewer students will be helped" (Breneman & Finn, 1978, p. 41). This is based on Breneman and Finn's assumption that an inequitable open access policy would deprive many students of the opportunity to enroll in their institution of choice, which would harm the private sector as most students would enroll in the public institutions. This means there is an association between "programs of federal cost-of-education allowances…with the amounts for each to be based on its enrollment of federally aided students" (Breneman & Finn, 1978, pp. 41–42). In this respect, Hartman argued that, "providing incentives to change state behavior in financing undergraduate education is the appropriate focus for federal policymakers troubled by the competitive disadvantage of private colleges and universities" (as cited in Breneman & Finn, 1978, p. 43). Agreeably, the President's Commission on Higher Education (1947) also stipulated that, "if education is to make the attainment of a more perfect democracy one of its major goals, it is imperative that it extend its benefits to all on equal terms" (p. 38, Vol. 1).

At this juncture, the author will now explore the Deweyian viewpoint on the relationship between progressive education and democratic governance for which open access to the educational experience is imperative.

John Dewey

1) _Necessity of Progressive Education and the Theory of Human Association Impacting on the Civic-Life Efficiency of Democratic Governance_:

In _Democracy and Education_, John Dewey (1916) hypothesized that democratic life is a self-renewing process that requires modes of human association for which the necessity of an educational experience is unavoidable. Dewey recognized this self-renewing process as the social continuity of life that can be experienced through progressive education and modes of human association which lie in the contribution that each person makes toward the improvement of ideal democratic governance. He, however, contended that "in the name of higher and more spiritual ideals, the arrangements for higher education have often not only neglected them, but looked at them with scorn as beneath the level of educative concern" (p. 119). For Dewey, this level of educative concern must be that which promotes civic-life efficiency or good citizenship with the capacity to share in a give and take of the democratic experience. Therefore, the democratic aim of progressive education is "to take part in correcting unfair privilege and unfair deprivation" (Dewey, 1916, 1997, pp. 119–120) so as to enable the citizenry to gain access to the ideal educational democratic experience.

Underlying this educational democratic experience, Dewey (1916) observed that people associate for a variety of purposes, which "grow and take shape through the process of social intelligence" (Dewey, 1938, p. 72) within the human community. This social intelligence is molded through social processes of human experience as the context of progressive education from which the individual's learning experience arises from the association of two principles—_continuity_ and _interaction_. The continuity "depends upon the quality of experiences" that influence one's future for better or for worse, and "education is the means of this social continuity of life" (Dewey, 1916, 1997, p. 2).

On the other hand, the interaction occurs through the reciprocity of the situational influence on one's experience, and thus, these two principles—*continuity* and *interaction*—are intimately connected to each other to provide the measure of educative significance and value of experience. This also implies that the democratic purpose of progressive education is to promote the freedom of social intelligence "since freedom resides in the operations of intelligent observation and judgment by which a purpose is developed, guidance given...to the exercise of...intelligence is an aid to freedom..." (Dewey, 1938, p. 71). In this case, the control mechanism in the development of social intelligence must maximize the ideal democratic freedom. This control mechanism, according to Dewey, is social control, which is enshrined "in the very nature of the work done as social enterprise in which all individuals have an opportunity to contribute and to which all feel a responsibility" (Dewey, 1938, p. 56).

2) *Democratic Ideal*:

Dewey (1938), moreover, recognized the interception of these two associational principles as generators of social control that set the criteria for the value of human experience and the progressive purpose of human potentiality. Thus, the overriding focus of this social control is the translation of individual learning experiences and potentialities into civic responsibilities while upholding the ideals of civil liberties. For this, Dewey (1916) posited that the criteria of the two elements of the associational principles "both point to *democracy*," which is "more than a form of government," since a democracy "is primarily a mode of associated living of conjoint communicated experience" (Dewey, 1916, 1997, pp. 86–87). Here, Dewey infers that the context of social continuity of life and human interaction is transmitted by the process of a communicated social experience that is educative in nature to form an ideal democratic life. This resonates with the standpoint of the President's Commission on Higher Education (1947) on the assertion that democracy demands an informed citizenry. As such, it must be perceived in the context of experiential learning that is characterized by modes of association for the ideal democratic conduct.

3) *Causal Modes of Human Associations*:

According to Dewey (1916), the modes of association reflect the variety of human associations that advance the socialization of group purpose within the array of social institutions, organizations, corporations, political parties, and community groups. Since there are varying degrees of human association, Dewey argues that society and community depict complex phenomena for which the power of democratic education bridges the gap to ensure cultural civility. From this standpoint, Dewey hypothesized that, "Any *education* given by a group tends to *socialize* its members, but the *quality of the socialization* depends upon the *habits and aims of the group*" (Dewey, 1916, 1997, p. 83). Thus, Dewey's theorization maintains that there is a causal relationship between the independent variable—*education*—and the dependent variable—*socialize*—"to the extent that changes in one variable are accompanied by systematic changes in the other(s)" (Singleton & Straits, 1988, p. 74). The manner of the systematic changes—*the quality of the socialization* as shown in Dewey's supposition—is dependent upon the intervening variable—*habits and aims of the group*. This is because "an intervening variable or mechanism linking the independent and dependent variables strengthens the causal inference" (Singleton & Straits, 1988, pp. 82 & 84)—which, in this case, is *the quality of the socialization of the group members.*

Dewey (1916) further suggested that there are two characteristics of the modes of association that must be measured to determine if improvement in the socialization of group members is necessary: (1) commonality of interest, and (2) some level of interaction and cooperation with other groups. In seeking this measure, two criteria must be considered: (1) How numerous and varied are the interests that are consciously shared? (2) How full and free is the interplay with other forms of association? The inquiry that underscores the parameters of these questions leads to the ideal of pragmatism for which the truth of a proposition is measured by its correspondence with experimental results and its practical outcome. Dewey believed that the democratic goal of education for both the individual and society as a whole must be based upon the quality of the learning experience and the understanding of the process of invigorating the educational experiences to allow people to fulfill their potential as members of society. The underlying premise here is what Dewey (1916) posited as shaping the democratic ideal that constitutes society, which is characterized by two traits: (1) Diversity and greater reliance upon shared mutual interests as factors in social control. (2) Free interaction that fosters change in social habits for continuous readjustment to meet renewed situational experience. Upholding this democratic ideal, the Report of President's Commission on Higher Education (1947) stressed:

> Democracy as a way of life uses varied institutional forms and changing patterns of cooperative association as time and circumstances may require, but it holds fast to its abiding elements: Its respect for human personality, its insistence on the fullest freedom of belief and expression for all citizens, its principle that all should participate in decisions that concern themselves, its faith in reason, its deep obligation to promote human well-being. These ideals and the processes through which they are translated into individual and social behavior must permeate American education from the nursery school through the highest reaches of the graduate and professional schools. (p.102, Vol. 1)

Consistent with Dewey and the President's Commission, Pinkney (1994 & 1997) contended that the situational experience requires democratic conditions and transitions favorable for the cooperative association in the ideal democratic governance. Therefore, the author will now examine the Pinkneyian tenets on the circumstances that are hostile to and of the transitional elements suitable to democratic governance, analyzing primarily the Ghanaian democratic culture.

This expository research is based on selected excerpts from *Democracy and Education*, by John Dewey. Copyright © 1916, by The Macmillan Company; copyright renewed © 1944 by John Dewey. Reprinted with permission of Scribner, an imprint of Simon & Schuster Adult Publishing Group.

Robert Pinkney

While the ideal of democracy has had remarkable success in many Western cultures, most notably in the United States of America, Robert Pinkney, in his 1994 work on *Democracy in the Third World*, explored the theoretical proposition and hostility toward democracy in developing countries. For the purpose of this thesis, concentration will be briefly focused on how the ideology of democracy has played in Ghanaian politics during the crucial periods leading to the country's independence in 1957, and more importantly, that which followed its transition from British colonial rule to its current multiparty rule of representative democracy. Also, there will be some insight into how these political conditions were shaped by the Ghanaian system of higher education. Here again, Pinkney's 1997 work on *Democracy and Dictatorship in Ghana and Tanzania* will be concurrently analyzed in terms of the different ideological tendencies of democracy in addressing the Ghanaian political system.

A) *Theory of Transition to Democracy*:

Transition to democracy, according to Pinkney, can be viewed from three perspectives: First, the undermining of a perceived authoritarian regime caused by factors of political instability, such as economic decline, intensified domestic and international pressures, decline in aid from the international communities, widespread corruption of the ruling party, and bureaucratic inefficiency. Pinkney emphasized that the overriding transitional factor to democracy in the Third World, for example Ghana, is the causal relationship between economic decline and authoritarian governments. Since in a causal relationship "all that one can observe is a constant or stable association between events" (as cited in Singleton & Straits, 1988, p. 79), Pinkney observed that Ghanaians became discontent due to escalating unemployment and the imminent rise of political forces challenging the authoritarian regime. Unlike authoritarian government, democracy, from the perspective of the President's Commission on Higher Education (1947), "is much more than a set of political processes. It formulates and implements a philosophy of human relations. It is a way of life—a way of thinking, feeling, and acting in regard to associations of men and groups, one with another" (p. 11, Vol. 1).

Second, the configuration of varied interests and demands of social groups, including formal political structures of society, have the propensity to stimulate a transition toward democracy. The underlying premise here is that the recognizable resources and enormous strength of interaction exist among these social groups, including religious institutions, universities, professional bodies, trade unions, and business organizations. More so, the political culture of the society tends to reflect the values, beliefs, and customs of these social groups to the extent that they may pose as a consolidated power toward conformity to the democratic ideal. Universities, for instance, served as the most effective social institutions in Ghanaian politics for the campaign toward democracy from 1966 to 1992. As noted by the President's Commission, the role of higher education as a social institution in a democratic society "is to provide a unified general education…find the right relationship between specialized training on the one hand, aiming at a thousand different careers, and the transmission of a common cultural heritage toward a common citizenship on the other" (President's Commission on Higher Education, 1947, p. 49, Vol. 1). However, no government in Ghana would have been able to survive for long without coming to terms with the chieftaincy, tribal rulers, or local governments (Pinkney, 1997).

The third transitional view to democracy involves the processes of conflict resolution and the consolidation of democracy that emerge in the context of consensus building between the opposing parties. In its democratic role for consensus building, higher education is expected "to serve as an instrument of social transition and its responsibilities are defined in terms of the kind of civilization society hopes to build" (President's Commission on Higher Education, 1947, p. 6, Vol. 1). As an instrument of social transition, higher education and the democratic elements of the society must concentrate on conflict resolution that focuses on areas such as: how the process of transition can be achieved, and the pace and magnitude at which it should occur. In respect to the process of consolidation of democracy, it should be recognized that a wide degree of consensus exists over the processes of resolving political conflict. Also, matters regarding the stability of the political system should be addressed, as well as the extensiveness of democracy in terms of scope for political participation. In addition, inquiry should be made as to how far an *elite veto* on democratic activity will go, as well as if there is, in fact, a *military* or *external veto* (Pinkney, 1997).

Reminiscing on these concerns, Pinkney (1997) conceived that "transitions, such as those in Ghana…based on government imposition, and moderate and gradual change, are more likely to lead to relatively stable democratic system, but subject to an elite veto and with only limited scope for broadening public participation" (p. 152). This means that stability of an ideal democratic form of government is dependent upon the break into elite vetoes and the rapid transitions that may stimulate democratic participation. It also calls for a clearer understanding of the nature of democracy that shapes these transitional processes toward democratic governance.

B) *The Nature and Types of Democracy*:

The nature of democracy, according to Pinkney (1994), "is elusive both as a concept and as a feasible objective" (p. 5). While the Pinkney tenets classified the concept of democracy into five ideological tendencies: (1) radical, (2) guided, (3) liberal, (4) socialist, and (5) consociational (Pinkney, 1994 & 1997), arguably, a sixth (6) category will be the populist paradigm.

C) *Radical and Guided Democracies*:

In terms of the radical democracy, Pinkney suggested this is the type for which society is seen as an aggregation of undifferentiated individuals exercising their rights and protecting their interests as active participants. Despite this, tyranny still exists among the majority. In a guided democracy, society is perceived as an *organic whole* with common interests. The ruling political party appears to execute the general will of the populace without being influenced by constitutional checks to protect the rights of the minorities (Pinkney, 1994 &1997).

D) *Liberal Democracy and Historical Ideologies in Ghanaian Democracy*:

In a liberal democracy, society is recognized as an aggregation of diverse citizens operating as both individuals and members of a social group with the commitment to representative democracy and the protection of varied interests. However, the underlying notion held in liberal democratic government, for instance, in Ghana, is that the state does not exist to execute the general will of the majority, which may be incompatible with the rights of minorities, but instead must conform to an organic whole. This way, the citizenry can enjoy some level of equity that upholds civil rights that is not necessarily social equity. This type of democratic government was prevalent during the then Gold Coast in the early post-war eras when the elite groups sought self-government and led to the formation of the United Gold Coast Convention (UGCC) of the Danquah-Busia liberal-wing in 1947-66. Within this period, however, the state socialist movement emerged when the late Dr. Kwame Nkrumah, the president of the First Republic of Ghana, became dissatisfied with the pace of the reformation efforts of the UGCC and broke away to form the Convention People's Party (CPP) in 1949.

E) *Socialist and Consociational Democracies, and Political Ideologies*:

The socialist democracy recognizes the active role of state government in the promotion of equality, social justice, redistribution of wealth through increased public or cooperative ownership, and extensive welfare provision, as well as the provision of a moral guide to political action. Consociational democracy, on the other hand, depicts the way in which a culturally diverse nation guarantees that all significant groups are represented within the government with none being frozen out by crude majoritaranism. It thus follows that in such a democratic system, society is viewed as consisting of distinctive groups based on language, race, or religion, but autonomous of one another and the state. Again, in such a system, the state only exists to act as a referee in the process of inter-group conflict and not to promote any utopian ideal such as socialism. While such a system exists in most African nations, it may be dominated by one of three ideological strands of state government: socialism, liberalism, and populism.

F) *Populist Democracy and Historical Trends in Ghanaian Political Ideologies*:

Populism, according to Pinkney (1997), "implies a suspicion of party politicians as a whole, and not just one-party regimes, as vehicles for articulating the popular will" (p. 40). Thus, party politicians are not viewed as representing the people, but instead as entrepreneurs who exploit the citizenry to win power and enrich themselves at the expense of the will of the populace. Since conditions such as governmental corruption, economic difficulties, and dissatisfaction with the military were conducive to a popular uprising through a *coup d'état*, an autocratic form of populist democracy emerged in Ghanaian politics from 1966 to 1992. Although within these periods Ghana briefly returned to multiparty democracy in the Second and Third Republics, for the most part, the military rule dominated the Ghanaian ideological democracies. For instance, contrary to popular democratic ideals, the armed forces of Ghana, led by Colonel (later Lieutenant General) E.K. Kotoka, in cooperation with the Ghana Police, staged a successful *coup d'état* in 1966, which overthrew the Nkrumah Government of the First Democratic Republic. Subsequent to this popular uprising in Ghanaian democratic politics, the National Liberation Council (NLC), under the Chairmanship of Lieutenant General J.A. Ankrah, assumed the reins of government, but was replaced in 1969 by Brigadier General (later Lieutenant General) A.A. Afrifa. This led to the Second Republic with Dr. Kofi Abrefa Busia of the Progress Party (PP) as Prime Minister, and in 1970, the former Chief Justice Edward Akuffo-Addo was elected President (Kludze, 1993; Pinkney, 1994 & 1997).

In 1972, General Acheampong of the National Redemption Council, which later became the Supreme Military Council (SMC), ousted the Busia Government. However, in 1978 Acheampong was also removed from office as Chairman of the SMC and Lieutenant General Akuffo became the Chairman of the ruling SMC. As corruption and mismanagement among military superiors escalated, another uprising of the junior officers led by Flight Lieutenant Jerry John Rawlings staged a coup in 1979, ending the rule of the Supreme Military Council, but was replaced by the Armed Forces Revolutionary Council (AFRC). After the previous corrupt military leaders had been tried by special courts without the right of appeal, the AFRC executed a number of the former heads of state, including other top military officials, by firing-squad, popular termed as a *house-cleaning* exercise. In this exercise, the AFRC ordered the arrest of some one hundred wealthy businessmen and former high-ranking officials, both military and civilian, who had occupied executive and managerial positions in the previous administrations. These arrests were justified on the claim that the individuals committed crimes with the intent of sabotaging the Ghanaian economy and mismanaging state funds, coupled with troubling corruption to the detriment of the Ghanaian people (Amnesty International News Release/Report, 1984; Kludze, 1993; & Pinkney, 1997).

However, since preparation was underway to restore Ghana to democratic governance, Dr. Hilla Limann of the People's National Party was elected President of the Third Republic in Ghana in 1979. After only two years in office, Flight Lieutenant Rawlings returned to power in 1981 in another *coup d'état*, overthrowing the People's National Party Government of Dr. Limann, and establishing the Provisional National Defense Council (PNDC). Due to the 1979 house-cleaning exercise, however, Flight Lieutenant Rawlings was, to some extent, perceived to be a more credible alternative leader than any civilian politician. The resurgence of the PNDC as a populist government was later viewed as the most authoritarian government in the history of Ghanaian democracy. For instance, Africa Watch and Amnesty International, two worldwide human rights organizations, reported several illegalities, brutalities, abuses, tortures, intimidations, arrests of innocent civilians, and political imprisonments and/or detentions of *prisoners of conscience* without trials (Africa Watch, 1989, & 1991; Amnesty International News Release/Report, 1984, 1985, & 1992 ; Kludze, 1993; & Pinkney, 1997).

Prisoners of conscience, from the perspective of Amnesty International, are those "persons imprisoned, detained or otherwise physically restricted by reason of their political, religious or other conscientiously held beliefs or by reason of ethnic origin, sex, color, or language, provided that they have not used or advocated violence" (Amnesty International, 1983, p. 3). Since the right to *habeas corpus* for political detainees was abolished by the PNDC in 1984 and replaced by decree of PNDC Public Order, these arrestees could not possibly receive fair trials. Some of these detainees were sentenced to death by Public Tribunals, while others, being unfairly tried, were also executed by decree of a Special Military Tribunal, consisting of approximately seven members of the Ghanaian Armed Forces. The PNDC government alleged that these individuals and prisoners of conscience were incited to overthrow the government. Also, the PDNC used its legislative powers to silence what it perceived as voices of political dissent, attacking the Ghana Bar Association, the press, and the trade unions, and later attempting to crack down on churches and other religious bodies through the imposition of a controversial PNDC Law 221. This new law required all religious organizations to register with the Ministry of the Interior to make them accountable to the government. However, the major Ghanaian religious bodies opposed the law on the premise that it constituted an infringement upon fundamental rights as guaranteed by the Universal Declaration of Human Rights (Africa Watch, 1989, 1990, 1991, & 1992; Amnesty International News Release/Report, 1984, 1985, 1990, 1991, & 1992; Kludze, 1993; & Pinkney, 1997).

G) *Contemporary Trends in Ghanaian Politics:*

Being faced with enormous foreign and domestic pressure, in which the Ghanaian universities and the International Monetary Funds (IMF) played a crucial role, the PNDC agreed to return Ghana to a representative democracy. The Ghana Bar Association (GBA) and the Ghanaian universities, represented by the National Union of Ghana Students (NUGS), insisted that a Constituent Assembly be popularly elected to draft a new Constitution. However, the PNDC government ignored their call and instead established a *Consultative Assembly*, composed of representatives from each District Assembly, the revolutionary organs, such as the Committee for the Defense of the Revolution (CDR), and other identifiable groups. Here again, some advocacy groups for true democratic governance, including the GBA and NUGS, denounced the Consultative Assembly as democratically unrepresentative and refused to send members. Despite this inaction on the part of the advocacy groups, the PNDC appointed a "Committee of Experts" to develop a draft constitution that was debated by the Consultative Assembly (Africa Watch, 1989, 1990 & 1991; Amnesty International News Release/Report, 1984, 1985 & 1990; Kludze, 1993).

Since a ban was placed on political party activities, only the PNDC government was able to campaign for the ultimate approval of the Constitution by a wide margin in a referendum held in 1992. Though the ban on political parties was lifted that same year, the registration process for political parties was too cumbersome to enable more competitive political campaigns for approximately two months for the general election scheduled for November 3, 1992. This gave the PNDC of Flight Lieutenant Rawlings, who had earlier retired from the Air Force to have an inequitable edge in the campaign, the victory in the presidential election with 55% of the vote. In spite of the widespread allegations of irregularities in the voting, the international observers invited by the PNDC concurred that the election was fair, and thus paved the way for Ghana to return to democratic governance in the Fourth Republic (Africa Watch, 1992; Amnesty International News Release/Report, 1991 & 1992; Kludze, 1993; Pinkney, 1994 & 1997). For an illustration, Table 1.1 displays the different ideological tendencies of democracy in Ghanaian Politics:

Table 1.1, Different Ideological Tendencies in Ghanaian Politics

STATE SOCIALIST	POPULIST	LIBERAL
Convention People's Party (CPP)—President Nkrumah (1949-66) of the First Republic.		United Gold Coast Convention (UGCC), National Liberation Movement (NLM), & the United Party (UP)—Danquah & Busia (1947-66)
National Alliance of Liberals (NAL)—Gbedemah & Agama (1969-72)		National Liberation Council (NLC)—Gen. Ankrah & Gen. Afrifa (1966-69), a military government.
		Progressive Party (PP)—Prime Minister Busia (1969-72) and President Akuffo-Addo of the Second Republic.
	National Redemption Council (NRC)/Supreme Military Council (SMC)—Gen. Acheampong & Gen. Akuffo (1972-79), a military government.	
People's National Party (PNP)—President Limann (1979-81) of the Third Republic.	Armed Forces Revolutionary Council (AFRC)—Ft. Lt. Rawlings (1979), a military government.	Popular Front Party (PFP)—Owusu (1979-81)
	Provisional National Defense Council (PNDC)—Ft. Lt. Rawlings (1981-92)	
National Convention Party (NCP)—Agykum (1992-Plus other extra-parliamentary parties)	National Democratic Congress (NDC)—President Rawlings (1992-2000) of the Fourth Republic.	New Patriotic Party (NPP)—President Boahen (2001-Present)

(Pinkney, 1997, p. 34).

Building on the crucial conditions and transitions conducive to democratic governance and the vital role that the Ghanaian universities played in this process, the author will now explore the editorial work of Murchland and associates as it applies to American institutions of higher learning.

This analysis is based on selected excerpts from *Democracy and Dictatorship in Ghana and Tanzania,* by Robert Pinkney, Copyright © 1997 by Macmillan Press Limited. Reproduced with permission of Palgrave Macmillan. The research is also based on selected excerpts from *Democracy in the Third World,* by Robert Pinkney, Copyright © 1994/2003 by Lynne Rienner Publishers, Inc. Reprinted with permission of the publisher.

The Editorial Work of Bernard Murchland and Associates

a) *Conceptual Scheme in the Democratic Governance of Higher Education*:

Concerned with the quest for answers to the shallowness of civic involvement in the U.S., Murchland, in his editorial work of 1991, provided insight into the democratic ideals that can shape growing public discourse. These essays show that Murchland's inquisition is intended to develop a *conceptual scheme* for understanding the practices of higher education in the process of American democratic governance. A conceptual scheme, according to Mark (1996), "is a way of understanding social work practice by categorizing people into groups…tie concepts together with assumptions and propositions…when they are well developed through, logic, or research—can also be called theories" (p. 5). In operationalizing his conceptual schemes, Murchland's concerns include seeking an answer as to what can be done to educate citizens for democratic society. Murchland also sought answers as to whether educators are correct in maintaining that they have been providing such an education. He was also interested in identifying the responsibilities of citizenship in a free society. In addition, Murchland inquired as to what American colleges are doing to fulfill the stated aims of citizenship education in their mission statements and as reflected in their catalogues. Finally, he wanted to find out whether colleges do, in fact, constitute a civic community.

b) *The Metaphor of the Marketplace in the Democratic Practices of Higher Education*:

In ascertaining answers to these conceptual schemes, Murchland hypothesized that democratic governance in higher education can be associated with the metaphor of market transactions for which the civic society is perceived as the producers and consumers more than as mere citizens. Murchland, moreover, believed that, "the metaphor of the marketplace powerfully shaped our self-understanding as a nation" (Murchland, 1991, p. 1). Congruent with Murchland's assumption, De

Groof, Neave, and Svec (1998) posited that the productive process of democratic education emphasizes duty and responsibility of higher education that espouse to the right of citizens' choice in compliance with the demands of the marketplace. They also contended that these marketplace demands reflect the balance of how higher education can act as a collective instrument for radical political reform on one hand and ultra-liberal view on the other to meet the economic and social priorities of a civic society. Perhaps in following up with this line of argument, when analyzing the Weberian ideology, Held (1987) also suggested that "Democracy is like the marketplace, an institutional mechanism to weed out the weakest and establish those who are most competent in the competitive struggle for votes and power" (p. 158).

Murchland's concept of the marketplace metaphor thus depicts the relationship between the role of higher education in educating for democratic citizenship/political education and its effects on civic responsibility of the citizenry. Murchland's assumption reflects compelling evidence that, for the most part, Americans and young people are increasingly alienated from our core democratic process. More importantly, he argued that while higher education professes to educate students for public service, social responsibility, and civic leadership, there is a great gap between the rhetoric and the reality of the commitment to those democratic ideals.

Furthermore, Murchland contended that although higher education has adapted to the notion of the marketplace metaphor in shaping the educational process for career skills development, it has, in fact, displaced other educational goals, including citizenship education. Since goal displacement constitutes a deficiency in operationalizing service objectives to achieve the program being desired (Neugeboren, 1991), Murchland (1991) stipulated that, "One wonders how educational institutions justify the rhetoric of their catalogue" (p. 2). On this note, and to reiterate, Murchland asked numerous questions: Do institutions of higher education really see the gap between what they claim and what they actually produce? Do students see it? Do colleges constitute a civic community? What can be done to educate citizens for a democratic society? Are educators correct in maintaining that they have been providing such an education? And in a more formal sense, what are colleges doing to fulfill the goals of citizenship education as stated in their catalogues? In response, Murchland's study indicated that, by and large, higher education offers students minimal education for democracy. This echoed Mathews's (in Murchland, 1991) assertion that the, "Academe lost interest in civic education centuries ago when thought was separated from action and the academic disciplines were born" (p. 49).

c) *Contemporary Aspect of Democratic Governance at Goddard College*:

While the magnitude of the controversy fueled by deep uncertainty and lack of interest in the civic mission of higher education for democratic education may be alarming (Barber in Murchland, 1991), a focused group study about the business and democracy at Goddard College showed other compelling evidence that upholds the ideal of democratic governance. Noted for its efforts to educate students through experiential learning, Goddard College is a progressive democratic institution in central Vermont that is committed to participatory democracy and egalitarian education (Schramm in Schapiro, 1999). Governed by this egalitarian purpose, Goddard's civic mission "is to advance the theory and practice of learning by undertaking new experiments based upon the ideals of democracy and on the principles of progressive education first asserted by John Dewey" (Schapiro, 1999, p. 17).

In operationalizing this civic mission, Goddard's programs share a common set of democratic actions, which include student-centered learning, problem-focused learning, integrative learning, teachers as facilitators, negotiated curriculum, study plans and learning contracts, authentic assessment, and work program or community service (Schapiro, 1999). In contrast, Murchland's study indicated that a vast majority of students do not associate the college's curriculum with citizenship education. Murchland, however, added that these students believed that there were fewer courses in government or public policy that tend to raise the concept of citizenship, but they also recognized that campus organizations, such as political clubs, fraternities, and student government, raise the awareness of democratic politics and engagement in community services (Murchland, 1991). Although the group study showed that the variety of program structures made governance and operational decisions at Goddard College involved a highly democratic process, they still lacked many appropriately designed organizational structures that place governance fully in the hands of the college community (Schramm in Schapiro, 1999).

d) *Alternatives for Civic Education*:

Consistent with Goddard College's civic mission program, Murchland's concern about what could be done to educate citizens for a democratic society pointed to four alternatives for civic education: 1) an effort to ensure civic literacy in order to understand the specification and principles on which democratic/political culture are based; 2) an approach to civic education that teaches civic values; 3) civic education that emphasizes civic skills for ideal democratic action and leadership; and 4) development of civic competence through commitment to social services and community projects (Mathews in Murchland, 1991). Murchland's study placed the responsibilities of citizenship in a free society into five categories: 1) the academic community's emphasis on civic knowledge of current events and the ways in which government works for productive members of society; 2) highest commitment to public service that addresses social problems; 3) emphasis on individualism since "citizenship is the responsibility of the individual student…means pursuing your own happiness without infringing on the rights of others" (p. 3); 4) the development of an active voice in the government of the individual's country or in shaping the values of society. The most troubling viewpoints of the students, pointed to 5) Voices of cynicism that express disappointment in the political processes of ideal democratic governance.

As to whether colleges do, in fact, constitute a civic community, the Murchland study showed opposing viewpoints: One group believed that colleges do constitute a civic community, while the other group did not recognize it as such, but acknowledged that there are some campus organizations that share the ideals of democratic association. Adding to this notion, Gutmann (in Murchland, 1991) posited that, "Universities serve democracy both as sanctuaries of non-repression and as associational communities. They also serve as gatekeepers of valuable social offices...they should give priority to the democratic principle of nondiscrimination over efficiency in their admissions procedures" (p. 77). Strengthening the Murchland and Gutmann tenets, Groof et al. (1998) and Schapiro (1999) argued that democracy is about governance, and the administration of higher education is the structure by which the governing system of democratic ideals thus constitutes a civic community. On this note, the author will now concentrate on the synthesis of the Breadth Theories, highlighting their differences and coherencies on democratic governance in the institutions of higher education.

This research is based on selected excerpts from *Higher Education and the Practice of Democratic Politics: A Political Education Reader,* edited and with an introduction by Bernard Murchland, Copyright © 1991 by the Kettering Foundation. Reproduced with permission of the publisher. The analysis is also based on selected excerpts from *Higher Education for Democracy: Experiments in Progressive Pedagogy at Goddard College, edited* by Steven A. Schapiro, Copyright © 1999 by Peter Lang Publishing Company. Reprinted with permission of the publisher.

PART 2

SYNTHESIS OF THE BREADTH THEORIES IN THE CIVIC MISSION OF HIGHER EDUCATION ADMINISTRATION

CHAPTER 2

EXPLORATION OF OPPOSING TENETS AND COHERENT ORIENTATION OF THE BREADTH THEORIES

1. *Administration of Democratic Governance in Higher Education and Group Interests:*

Democratic governance, according to Schramm (in Schapiro, 1999), is "a system that governs many people requires definitions, rules, organizational bodies, regulations, and procedures, etc. to spell out the terms and arrangements that makes up the governance contract" (p. 259). Schramm adds that, "these formal agreements define the democratic governance system and provide the structure of democracy, the framework within which democracy operates" (p. 259). However, Benjamin and his associates (1950), and McDonnell, Timpane & Benjamin (2000) conceived the administration of democratic governance in higher education as the most practical instrument for educating people in the ways of achieving freedom. They believed that the essence of freedom is the core objective of the existence of a democratic college or university. While not focusing specifically on higher education, but primarily on general education, Dewey (1916, 1997 & 1938), for the most part, perceived the essence of freedom as responsive to the conditions favorable to the intellectual development of the individual toward independence and social responsibility. However, just like the Benjamin stance, Dewey also recognized a causal relationship between democratic education and human freedom. Consistent with the Murchland's (1991) editorial work of Mathews's argument on civic intelligence, for Dewey, the administration of democratic governance must allow intellectual freedom, the interaction of diverse potentiality, and group interests in the educational process (Dewey, 1916, 1997 & 1938).

Argued in Murchland (1991), Mathews conjectured that, "If colleges and universities are responsible for the development of the minds of their students, then they are certainly responsible for those particular modes of rationality that are civic" (p. 55). Mathews's position is that the development of civic intelligence should be comprehensive to the connectedness of shared interests in capacity building for civic responsibility. In this regard, Mathews contended that, "If the civic affairs (politics) involve more than influencing governments, then that responsibility requires a reconsideration of even our best efforts to prepare the next generation for public life" (in Murchland, 1991, p. 55). Echoing this notion, the President's Commission on Higher Education (1947) stipulated that the democratic responsibility of the institutions of higher education should be responsive to the emerging change in the social and economic needs of the populace. They must also focus the training of the citizenry to be responsible for providing the solution to social problems and for the administration of public affairs.

2. _Democratic Governance in Higher Education and Public Policy Interests:_

On the contrary, Breneman and Finn (1978) felt that due to escalating tuition costs, which preclude many people from pursuing college degrees, the democratic interest of higher education should be directed toward public financial support for access to college admissibility. They argued that in the administration of democratic governance, public "policy should be responsive to society's overall interests in the nature, scope, and purposes of higher education as it approaches a decade or more of limited growth or retrenchment" (p. 413). From a somewhat consistent perspective with the Breneman and Finn (1978) concern about the impasse caused by retrenchment, Pinkney (1997) speculated that a retrenchment is likely to weaken at least three of the government's major power bases: 1) beneficiaries of government patronage, such as public servants and contractors, will suffer due to lost jobs; 2) urban poor will suffer due to the reduction in social services, increased rates of unemployment, and economic inflation; and 3) the productive sector of the economy that is susceptible to government control will depend more on market forces than on favorable government intervention. Agreeing with the Breneman and Finn (1978) tenets, Cook (1998) claimed that because of the sheer impact of colleges' financial management, higher education thus constitutes a policy community that favors redistribution of public resources to alleviate tuition burden of the citizenry. Cook pointed out that the policy interests of higher education administration reflect the gravity of citizens' interest for involvement in public policy advocacy in funding educational projects.

3. *Radical Democratic Governance and Complexity of Group Interests:*

Like Dewey (1916, 1997 & 1938) and Murchland (1991), Pinkney (1994) believed that because group interest is complex, and because government must retain the support of these interests in order to survive, the administration of democratic governance is quite unusual in the contemporary world. Pinkney (1997), however, theorized that the "increase in deprivation, coupled with reduced government ability to mitigate its effects, may lead to the formation of a variety of self-help and protest groups which may ultimately provide fertile ground for opposition parties" (p. 142). Pinkney (1994) further professed that the network of influential groups, for instance, in the Third World is generally less extensive, and the assertiveness of the citizenry wanting to safeguard its rights against oppression of the radical masses is lower. For this, Pinkney argued that some governments have, in effect, been able to claim a mandate from the majority to pursue radical reforms, even if it meant subverting the interests of minorities or treating them harshly, and/or imprisoning those who opposed such ideological reform.

Noted in Pinkney's 1997 work, these radical democratic interests were, by and large, prevalent during the Ghanaian dictatorial regimes, as can be noted during the military rule of Generals Kotoka, Afrifra, Acheampong, Akuffo, and the then Flight Lieutenant Rawlings. Nonetheless, Pinkney (1994) pointed out that this radical form of government can be destabilized if democratic governance upholds the institutionalized system of checks and balances of a civic society. Pinkney added that in the absence of adequate institutionalization that legitimatizes the ideal democratic system, governments tend to resort to authoritarianism. Unlike Pinkney (1994 & 1997), in Benjamin (1950), Taylor perceived a radically democratic administration as an instrument of morale and efficiency suitable for civic reform. Taylor argued that until faculty, students, and administration are given the freedom, power, and responsibility to make policies toward civic engagement, there will be no shared democratic experience in higher education. For Taylor, a radically democratic administration is the model of governance that can induce such an ideal reform since it operates within an experiential learning process for innovation.

4. *Structure of Democratic Governance in Higher Education Administration:*

Quite the opposite, in Schapiro (1999), Schramm's contention indicates that Taylor's (in Benjamin, 1950) postulations will only hold on the basis of a democratic structure that favors a representative form of government. Schramm suggested that the structure of a democratic government in higher education administration can be categorized into two sections: 1) a hierarchical board to president-to-management decision-making structure; and 2) a participatory faculty-student-staff democratic classroom, community meeting, and College Executive Committee decision structure. The underlying premise of Schramm's categorization is that it is the decision-making process that defines the operation of these democratic structures in addressing the complex interests of the college community. According to Schramm, the decision-making process within organizations can be grouped into four categories: a) ownership and governance decisions; b) management and administrative decisions; c) operational decisions; and d) individual/constituency decisions. He cautioned, however, that in the absence of a democratically elected administration, authority, accounta-bility, and information become largely one-way flows in a hierarchical structure as illustrated in Figure 2.1 below.

Figure 2.1, Hierarchical Government Structure

(Schramm in Schapiro, 1999, p. 267).
Reprint adapted from *Higher Education for Democracy: Experiments in Progressive Pedagogy at Goddard College,* edited by Steven A. Schapiro. Copyright © 1999 by Peter Lang Publishing, Inc. Reprinted with permission from the publisher.

In Benjamin (1950), Taylor, on the other hand, argued that the struc-ture and decision-making process in a democratic administration "is organic and not linear" (p. 43). Taylor added that in such a system, the governing body is diverse in its representation, and by the granting of powers, bestows upon the college community the right of self-government with the responsibility for advancing the general welfare and stability of the institution. More so, the working committees consist of joint faculty-trustee-staff committees, and information is shared, although dissemination of decisions may take a radical approach so that they may be implemented. Therefore, it does not really matter if the process of democratic governance is radically administered since the civic objective and the complex interests of the college community are addressed.

However, Schramm (in Schapiro, 1999) argued that the best interests of the people are truly served in an administration that has the most suitable democratic governance structure. He added that to ensure that there is a participatory form of democratic governance, the interests of the majority should reflect a circular structure of decision-making in its political process. Schramm posited that in a participatory democratic governance structure, members serve as stakeholders in the organization and the authority becomes circular, from organization members to board to management members. Accountability also becomes circular, from members to management to board to members. Therefore, there is no role ambiguity since the circularity provides clarity about roles while affording more equity in relationships and encouraging a flow of information in all directions, among members, board, and management as illustrated in Figure 2.2.

Figure 2.2, Democratic Governance Structure

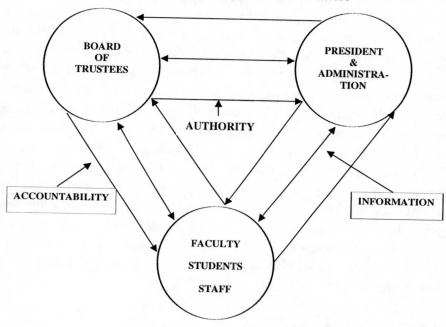

5. *Conflicts Inherent in the Political Processes of Democratic Governance:*

Although to some degree, Pinkney's (1994 & 1997) assumption of the complexity of group interests agrees with the other Breadth Theories, with the exception of that of Breneman and Finn (1978), he also maintained that the interaction between the various group interests and demands of the political structures tend to generate conflicts in the political processes of a civic society. The political processes, from the Pinkney (1994) perspective, reflect the framework within which different political ideologies inform or catalyze political actions or persuasions in the context of democratic governance. Inconsistent with the Pinkney's supposition, for Dewey (1916), are human associations that isolate themselves from full and free interplay with other modes of association conflict with the political processes of a civic society. According to Dewey (1916 & 1938), it is instead the various group interests that are consciously communicated and shared in the context of experiential learning induced by the continuity of group interaction, and thus they constitute a desirable framework for democratic governance. This communicated learning experience that molds social intelligence through the interplay of varied interests, from the Deweyian tenet, is what Benjamin and his associates (1950), Murchland and his associates (1991), and the President's Commission on Higher Education (1947) refer to as democratic/civic education. Dewey's (1916, 1997 & 1938) contention is that the potentialities of democratic education should recognize the collective interests of human associations and should be directed toward the development of social intelligence. This social intelligence, however, should also be connected to the learning possibilities inherent in ordinary experience.

6. _Democratic Education and Divergent Group Interests:_

Mathews (in Murchland, 1991) argued that, "An education for politics is necessarily an education in the practice of making choices with others who are different from us" (p. 54). While Mathews's tenet is consistent with the other Breadth Theories, he disagreed with the Pinkney's (1994 & 1997) conjectures on the negative notion about the emergence of conflicts inherent in the complexity of group interests. Mathews, for instance, professed that civic education occurs when making diverse choices and the conflicts inevitable when making such choices produce the necessary pressure that leads the citizenry to learn and develop social intelligence toward civic responsibility. Similar to the other Breadth Theories, with the exception of Pinkney, who did not explicitly make this connection, in Murchland (1991), Gutman also observed a causal relationship between democracy and democratic education within the context of the conflicts associated with the complexity of group interests. However, Cook's (1998) contention tends to agree with the Pinkney (1994 & 1997) arguments regarding the effect of the inherent conflicts associated with divergent group interests. Cook's (1998) assertion is that the administration of democratic governance in higher education of varied interests with greater internal conflicts can face difficulty when it comes to shaping public policy. But, arguing with the other like-minded Breadth Theories, Cook posited that when there is cohesiveness in the varied interests of the administration of democratic governance in higher education, the group interests will serve as a vital resource for influencing public policy agendas, decisions, and their ultimate implementation for the public good.

7. *Conditions Conducive to Democratic Developments, National Developments, and Societal Civility*:

In spite of his (1994 & 1997) differences with the other Breadth Theories about the connection with the varied interest of groups' conflicts, Pinkney (1994), like Benjamin (1950 & 1965), observed that there is a correlation between democratic developments and national developments. As an observed correlation, Pinkney and Benjamin are inferring that "one of the two variables" (democratic and national developments) "is related to the other in some way" (Triola, 2002, p. 434). There are, however, some slight differences in their tenets: While Benjamin associated the observed correlation in terms of the role of higher education and national development, Pinkney claimed that there are exceptions to this correlation. According to Benjamin (1965), "The kind of education in general, and of higher education in particular, which a country needs and can use is closely related to the course and level of the country's development" (p. 3). Pinkney (1994), on the other hand, contended that, "Countries in Eastern Europe achieved many other developments without democracy…and where democracy and other developments have gone together, the pace has been uneven" (p. 19). He, however, added that a nation void of democratic governance will most likely have no checks and balances, and this can strengthen authoritarianism at the expense of democracy. Therefore, according to

Pinkney's observation, at least seven conditions are conducive to demo-cratic governance and national developments, as indicated in Table 1.2, but there are problems associated with those ideals.

Table 1.2, Conditions Conducive to Democracy

Conditions	Supporting authors	Arguments	Problems
Economic development	Lipset (1959)	Correlation exists between wealth and democracy; increased national wealth makes competition for resources less desperate.	1) Correlation is not the same as cause. 2) Greater wealth may strengthen the resources of authoritarian rulers. 3) Process and rapidity of economic growth is not specified clearly.
Political attitudes and behavior	Almond and Verba (1963)	Democracy requires a willingness to accept government by consent as a means of resolving conflict.	Attitudes may be shaped by social and economic circumstances.
Inter-elite relations	Rustow (1973)	Democracy emerges when elites agree to the rules of the political game rather than risk national disintegration; these rules can subsequently be adapted to accommodate non-elites.	1. Why is a point reached where national unity is preferred to violent conflict or disintegration? 2. How can elite attitudes be ascertained?
Social structures and interaction between social groups	Moore (1967)	Democracy is most likely to evolve where the monarchy checks the power of the nobility, and the aristocracy goes into commerce.	How to explain the existence of democracy in countries with a diversity of social antecedents.

Political institutions	Heper (1991), Stephens (1989)	Democracy requires the development of institutions (especially pressure groups and political parties) which can filter public demands and thus facilitate compromise.	1. Danger of historical determinism. 2. Role of economic changes, external influences, and even society, not clear.
Sequences in development	Binder *et al.* (1971), Dahl (1971)	Democracy is easier to establish if political competition precedes mass participation, and if major conflicts over the role of the state are resolved one at a time.	1. Danger of historical determinism. 2. Problems of recognizing and qualifying the variables.
External influences	Seldom offered as a principal explanation	Foreign governments, institutions or individuals may supply ideas, offer inducements, or apply sanctions.	Influence can only be indirect; democracy cannot be imposed.

In terms of the democratic developments, Pinkney (1994) theorized that there are two inter-related variables: (1) the nature of indigenous political culture; and (2) the relationship between the state and civil society. Benjamin (1950 & 1965), McDonnell, Timpane, & Benjamin (2000), Dewey (1916 & 1938), the editorial work of Murchland (1991), and Pinkney (1994 & 1997) conceived the nature of the indigenous political culture as pertaining to the societal democratic institutions that are responsive to the indigenous demands of democratic governance. Pinkney, for example, claimed that the emergence of democratic institutions stems from the rising concerns about social causes and the conflicts inherent in the decision-making processes that address societal concerns. Paramount among these institutions, Benjamin (1950 & 1965), and McDonnell & Benjamin (2000) argued that it is the role of higher education to shape societal and economic securities, and to prepare the citizenry for active participation in the democratic process and social responsibility. Benjamin added that colleges and universities must serve as active forces within the community, producing a cultured citizenry, and addressing those safety concerns that are crucial toward meeting the inalienable rights, the pursuit of freedom, and the happiness of the populace. According to Benjamin (1965), "A ruling class that is committed to first-level security and first-level productivity is also tied to first-level education, whether aware of it or not" (p. 5).

However, like Dewey (1916) and Murchland and his associates (1991), Benjamin suggested that the content of democratic education should reflect the experiences of the learners and be transmitted in accordance to its function as part of the social fabric. It is this social fabric that the Breadth Theories conceived as the indigenous infrastructure suitable for citizens' adaptation, democratic living, and effective democratic governance. In this respect, the President's Commission on Higher Education (1947) cautioned that, "Colleges must accelerate the normally slow rate of social change which the educational system reflects," since "education is the foundation of democratic liberties," and "without an educated citizenry alert to preserve and extend freedom, it would not long endure" (pp. 23 & 25, Vol. 1). They added that, "we need to find ways quickly or making the understanding and vision of our most farsighted and sensitive citizens the common possession of all our people" (p. 23).

Therefore, Dewey (1916, 1997) contended that, "the failure to realize that the functional development of a situation alone constitutes a *whole* for the purpose of mind is the cause of false notions which have prevailed in instruction concerning the simple and the complex" (p. 199). Dewey believed that just as social intelligence is shaped by the learning experiences of human associations, so, too, is democracy formed by the aggregates of *a posteriori* (after the fact) experiences in human interactions. Similar to the Deweyian (1916 & 1934) tenets and Benjamin (1950 & 1965) arguments in Murchland (1991), Gutman also observed a causal relationship between democratic education and freedom of the citizenry within the context of fostering societal civility. Affirming this observation, Gutman averred:

> Democratic education is therefore a political as well as an educational ideal....Democratic education supplies the foundations upon which a democratic society can secure the civil and political freedoms of its adult citizens without placing their welfare or its very survival at great risk. In the absence of democratic education, risks—perhaps even great risk—will still be worth taking for the sake of respecting the actual preferences of citizens, but the case for civic and political freedom and against paternalism is weaker in a society whose citizens have been deprived of an adequate education. Democracy thus depends on democratic education for its full moral strength. (pp. 68, 78–79)

8. *Relationship Between the State and Civil Society*:

Regarding the relationship between the state and civil society, like Breneman and Finn (1978), in Benjamin (1950), Haskew perceived it as the philanthropic responsibility of ensuring that state policy favors adequate financial aid for the pursuit of college education. Haskew conceived that grants-in-aid should be provided freely in order to counteract the antidemocratic impact of financial barriers to college admissibility. He maintained that a philanthropic responsibility of state's financial support to college reflects the "expression of brother-care-for-brother that is the foundation-stone of democracy" (p. 159). Also, he argued that it is antidemocratic to preserve the propriety interests of some at the expense of society at large, since by providing free access to higher education can contribute to the interests of the civic society.

Consistent with the Haskew's argument, Breneman and Finn (1978) also posited that "Encouraging interstate portability of subsidies appears to be one logical means of developing a national system of colleges and universities and of diversifying educational offerings open to students" (p. 418). They added that in higher education, the philanthropic responsibility contributes to pedagogical excellence and encourages bold innovation. Affirming the benefits of state's philanthropy, responsibility, and consequences for not heeding to these notions, the President's Commission on Higher Education (1947) also declared:

> Under the pressure of rising costs and of a relative lessening of public support, the colleges and universities are having to depend more and more on tuition fess to meet their budgets. By allowing the opportunity for higher education to depend so largely on the individual's economic status, we are not only denying to millions of young people the chance in life to which they are entitled; we are also depriving the Nation of a vast amount of potential leadership and potential social competence which it sorely needs. (pp. 28–29, Vol. 1)

On the other hand, Dewey (1916 & 1938) and Murchland and his associates (1991) conceived the relationship between the state and civil society as pertaining to the value of community democratic experience. According to Dewey, democracy can only be understood in the context of community experience through communication, and only by understanding democracy will the citizenry understand the type of community in which moral education can be fully realized. Dewey's contention is that community experience is valuable and provides the theory of democratic living. Therefore the quality of this democratic living must be judged by the effect that the community experience has on the individual's present and future, and the extent to which the individual is able to contribute to society. It means the relationship between the state and civic society signifies the structure of communal life whereby the political life and democratic way of living can be expressed. Dewey posited that once the theory of experience is acquired, educators can set about progressively organizing the democratic subject matter in a way that takes account of students' past experiences. This provides the participants of this democratic education with the experiences that will continue to open up, rather than shut down, their future experiences and contribution to the civic society.

Strengthening Dewey's position, Murchland and his associates (1991) claimed that political community presupposes differences in experience, but communal life is developed to appreciate and sustain those differences and provide the context for which they can be expressed. The expression of these learning experiences energizes the responsibility of citizenship because citizenship implies civic participation in the political processes of the society. More so, human association requires politics because it is through politics that the community determines the criteria for the dissemination of values among the civic society. On the contrary, Pinkney (1997) contended that the ideology of the political context that bridges the state-civic association can be hostile toward the ideal of democratic participation. For instance, an authoritarian state can stunt independent political participation, and the coercive civic society can render such participation futile. He observed that, "An over-bearing state which attempts to control every aspect of political life, as in the totalitarian model, and a weak state which is unable to convert popular demands into policy outputs, can both be equally harmful to democracy" (p. 24).

As can be seen, apart from their cohesiveness, for the most, the synthesis of the Breadth Theories has also shown some opposing viewpoints. Therefore, the researcher will evaluate these Breadth Theories to ascertain the premises of their strengths and weaknesses to uphold the vitality of their interconnectedness.

PART 3

EVALUATION OF THE BREADTH THEORIES IN THE DEMOCRATIC GOVERNANCE OF HIGHER EDUCATION

CHAPTER 3

CONSTRUCTIVE ASSESSMENT OF THE IDEOLOGIES OF THE BREADTH THEO-RIES IN DEMOCRATIC GOVERNANCE

a) *Democratic Governance in Higher Education Administration and Retrenchment Policy*:

The underlying premise of democratic governance in higher education administration, for which the Breadth Theories tried to assert, contends that the mandate for civic education exemplifies the democratic action of higher education (Benjamin, 1950 & 1965; McDonnell, Timpane, & Benjamin, 2000; Dewey, 1916, 1997 & 1938; Groof et al., 1998; Hickey, Voorhees and Associates, 1969; Murchland, 1991; & Schapiro, 1999). However, the Breneman and Finn (1978), and Pinkney (1994 & 1997) tenets were quite flaccid in establishing this connection for democratic governance in higher education administration. Breneman and Finn, for instance, were more concerned about retrenchment policy on students' financial aid, along with its impact on open access, and enrollment management in higher education. Though their arguments were credible, unlike Pinkney (1997), they fell short of establishing the manner in which this retrenchment policy weakens the process of democratic governance. It should, however, be noted that Pinkney's contention on the retrenchment policy is also not based on financial aid policy per se, but in relation to its impact on the elements of transition to democratic governance.

b) *Free Enterprise System*:

What seems to have weakened the Breneman and Finn (1978) stance is the argument that, due to the distinctive features of the free enterprise system that characterizes the public and private institutions of higher education, not every venture may be successful. As noted, Breneman and Finn were speaking about potential anonymities surrounding guaranteed equal access to federal funds, which unfortunately tend to favor public colleges over private institutions. Even though their postulations were most convincing, the free enterprise system is believed to be beneficial to every individual and institution. A free market economy is a system endowed with an enormous economic liberty of operation, educational opportunity, and price systemizing, as well as a high degree of transaction that allows voluntary interaction among individuals and institutions for mutual benefits (Grigsby, 1999; Maddox & Lilie, 1984).

Although the Breneman and Finn contention on the obscurities of the free enterprise system is somewhat weak, they made a strong case regarding the disparity in tuition rates that exists between public and private higher education sectors. Moreover, as they suggested, the Report of the Web-based Education Commission (2000) also indicated that average tuition and fees at public colleges have risen 44% and the average at private colleges have risen 40% after adjusting for inflation. Nonetheless, one study signifies that new technologies are transforming postsecondary institutions. College enrollment administrators are beginning to use technology as a cost effective mechanism to meet the escalating crisis in higher education spending, as well as to accommodate the exploding enrollment of both prospective and returning students. Interestingly, privatization of higher education indicates that the profit-making sector sees education as an investment opportunity. A growing number of for-profit e-learning institutions are emerging, thus providing students with alternatives to public education. Also, close to 500,000 foreign students currently study in the U.S., and more importantly, global demand for higher education is forecasted to reach 160 million students in 2025 (Web-based Education Commission, 2000).

c) *Commonality of Interests among the Public and Private Higher Education Sectors:*

Despite Breneman and Finn's (1978) murky argument about the free enterprise system, yet well-founded on the disparity issue, they also concluded that irrespective of the complex varied interests within the higher education community, on most federal policy issues its interests are not much different between the public and private institutions. Thus, the complex varied interests tend to bridge commonality of interests among the public and private higher education sectors. Supporting the Breneman and Finn point of view, Cook (1998) went a step further in alluding that the commonality of interests is a standard democratic model against which interest groups are judged since it constitutes a common cause. The common cause, according to Cook, "provides a good example of the way that member-based organization actually operates...association leaders do agenda-setting in conjunction with the activists college and university...approve key decisions...do the implementation and exercise other discretionary authority..."(pp. 98–99). Adding to this common cause notion, the President's Commission on Higher Education (1947) concurred:

> Education has taught the concept of common humanity and brotherhood; the schools and colleges have tried to create world understanding; teachers have presented the ideal of peace and cooperation among men and nations....The ends of democratic education in the United States will not be adequately served until we achieve a unification of our educational objectives and processes. American education must be so organized and conducted that it will provide, at appropriate levels, proper combinations of general and special education for students of varying abilities and occupational objectives. (pp. 19, 62–63, Vol. 1)

d) *Cause-and-Effect Relationship in the Transition to Democratic Governance*:

Unlike Breneman and Finn (1978) and Cook (1998) on the commonality of interests, Pinkney (1994 & 1997) viewed complex varied interests as constituting conflicts that make the administration of democratic governance atypical in a civil society. By this viewpoint, Pinkney may be suggesting a cause-and-effect relationship in the transition to democratic governance, since "a causal relationship…is something inferred from an observed association between events" (Singleton and Straits, 1999, p. 79). While from Pinkney's tenet it may seem weak in making the case for a cause-and-effect relationship, he, in fact, observed that there were swinging transitions to democratic governance in Ghanaian politics until the country's apparent stability with the Fourth Republic. For this, Pinkney (1997) hypothesized that, "Ghana emerged from colonial rule with a strong civil society, that the CPP (Convention People's Party) empowered that society by imposing state control over previously autonomous institutions, and that society has never really recovered, hence the failure of attempts to establish a democratic order" (p. 66).

In Pinkney's view, the obvious instability of democratic order in Ghanaian history can be traced from the argument that while the socialist ideology of the CPP government upheld the value of civil society gained from colonial government, its preference to statehood was antagonistic to the ideals of institutional autonomy. He, moreover, observed that during Ghana's colonial rule, the democratic form of government that shaped its civil society involved the principles of autonomy held by its democratic institutions. As noted by Held (1987), principles of autonomy provide the crucial conditions that enable citizens to pursue their self-interests, uphold the rule of law, and protect and support individual liberty and rights. These autonomy principles are in alignment with the ideal of a civil society, which is "premised on the recognition that the general good can only be realized through the enforcement of law and the conscious direction of the state" (in Held, 1987, p. 116).

The question then arises: The CPP government had a strong commitment to a civil society and imposition of state control, so why did the attempts to establish a democratic order fail? In answering this, Pinkney (1997) strongly contended that political and social infrastructures have the ability to strengthen or weaken the attempts toward stable democracy. Pinkney's contention may seem troubling since the social infrastructures, which are perceived to be vital systems for the democratic ideal, based on his assertion, can also weaken democratic governance. However, he convincingly alluded that even though these infrastructures may be strong to the extent that they can regulate tensions in the political system and curtail the magnitude of governmental powers, each structure can also retain its own role and self-interests with the likelihood of causing destabilization in the democratic process. For example, Pinkney observed that in Ghana, on the whole, the contexts of party conflict since 1992 have not been conducive to a pluralist form of democracy. There is therefore a need for other political and social groups to develop and consolidate the democratic process.

From the Pinkney standpoint, this need also reflects the widely held belief that, "democracy functioned more effectively if there were adequate autonomous institutions in society which could bridge the gap between government and governed" (Pinkney, 1997, p. 62). Pinkney (1997) further argued that in the absence of such autonomous institutions, there will be an emergence of a totalitarian policy in which there is incongruence between the values and beliefs of the government and those of the populace. Cognizant with these viewpoints, and as one of the autonomous democratic institutions, the President's Commission on Higher Education (1947) posited that the civic objectives of higher education must provide an experiential education for students:

> To develop for the regulation of one's personal and civic life a code of behavior based on ethical principles consistent with democratic ideals. To participate actively as an informed and responsible citizen in solving the social, economic, and political

problems of one's community, State, and Nation....The effectiveness of any general education program will depend on the
quality and attitudes of those who administer and teach it. (pp.
50–51, & 60, Vol. 1)

Although to some extent, Pinkney failed "to prove that democracy
was, in fact, the result of a process of cause and effect" (p. 19), he did,
however, argue that, "democracy itself might be a cause rather than
effect of reconciliation between groups" (p. 24). Strikingly, Pinkney
assumed that democracy may be established for reasons other than
groups' interests, favoring reconciliation in matters such as insistence
of a departing colonial power or military government and opposition
groups so as to work within an ideal democratic framework. Thus,
Pinkney seems to reaffirm the tenet that transition to stable democratic governance can only be safeguarded when it is responsive to the
complex interest of the society, as opposed to merely a group. So then,
to what extent can the administration of democratic governance be
successful in contemporary higher education? Though Dewey (1916 &
1938) and Murchland and his associates were somewhat responsive to
this question, Benjamin and his associates (1950) were the only
Breadth theorists to explicitly answer it. They suggested that the
degree of success will depend upon the qualities of higher culture and
progressive strength that shape the democratic purposes among
higher education administration toward security management and
national development. The premise for security management in the
democratic governance of higher education administration entails an
institutional commitment to educational programs that can enhance
the knowledge base of service-learners to uphold the development of
higher culture for which the citizenry is exposed to basic knowledge in
the management of the affairs of homeland security. The ideology of
the development of civic virtues for higher culture in the democratic
governance of civic society exemplifies one of the social fabrics of
good citizenship for ensuring homeland security at the face of growing regional or tribal conflicts, civic unrests, and the terror threats of

radical religious fanatics in the world community. It can thus be put forward that this higher culture characterizes the social and civic responsibilities that should be channeled to the citizenry, and in effect, distinguishing the progressive strength of higher education's democratic action toward security measures and national development.

e) *Causality of Democratic Education in National Development*:

From the standpoint of the editorial work of Benjamin (1950), Hornbake associated the higher culture of societal civility with the degree of democratic education that one acquires through the sheer democratic actions induced to the community of learners by the institutions of higher education. Hornbake saw the direction of this causal relationship on "the hypothesis that democracy requires an indigenous education. A person so educated is cultured. A person not so educated is lacking culture. But culture is indigenous to a social order" (in Benjamin, 1950, pp. 188 & 200). From the Hornbake's hypothesis, the causal reference to *democracy* may serve as an antecedent variable, "which is causally prior to both the independent and dependent variable, and thus, can produce a spurious relationship" (Singleton & Straits, 1998, p. 82).

However, as Singleton and Straits pointed out, "Social scientists generally require at least three kinds of evidence to establish causality. These requisites are association, direction of influence, and nonspuriousness" (p. 79). That means the inherent inference of a spurious relationship should be eliminated from the Hornbake's hypothesis otherwise the requisite for nonspuriousness cannot be established. Notably, the overriding causal relationship to which the Hornbake's hypothesis is pointing is the independent—presumed indigenous education—and the dependent—presumed indigenous culture—associating to an anticipated extraneous variable—the democratic social order of societal civility. While in most cases the extraneous variable is held constant, or may be categorized as controlled and/or uncontrolled (Singleton & Straits, 1998), the anticipated democratic social order of societal civility is implied in Hornbake's hypothesis as a common extraneous variable. This analogy underpins Singleton and Straits (1998) prediction that:

> If two variables happen to be related to a common extraneous variable, then a statistical association can exist if there is no inherent link between the variables. Therefore, to infer a causal relationship from an observed correlation there should be good reason to believe that there are no "hidden" factors that could have created an accidental or spurious relationship between the variables. When an association or correlation between variables cannot be explained by an extraneous variable, the relationship is said to be nonspurious. When a correlation has been produced by an extraneous third factor, and neither of the variables involved in the correlation has influenced the other, the relationship is called a spurious relationship. (pp. 80–81)

f) *Democratic Governance as a Posteriori of Mode of Associated Progressive Experience*:

Dewey (1916 & 1938), on the other hand, viewed the success of democratic governance as *a posteriori* of mode of associated progressive experience developed within the context of social intelligence and democratic community. Dewey seemed interested in a democratic community because he strongly believed that education and democracy are intimately connected, but can be developed through experiential learning. For Dewey, good education should have both a societal purpose as well as a purpose for the individual student. He persuasively argued that educators (that also means higher education) have a responsibility to provide students with experiences that are immediately valuable and that better enable students to contribute to civic society. For this reason, Dewey indubitably objected a predetermined and *a priori* context of experience, and instead defended his position for *a posteriori* experience. However, one may wonder how *a posteriori* learning experience can be acquired without having to begin with *a priori* potential to learn, since, according to Socrates, "all learning is recollection of knowledge innate in the soul" (Plato, 1981, pp. 1–2). More so, a recollection process can thus be associated with the Dewey's progressive experience notion, which therefore makes Dewey's rejection of *a priori* learning experience somewhat baseless.

g) *Civic Education Versus Civic Intelligence in Democratic Governance*:

Concomitant with the Dewey's (1916 & 1938) argument for *a posteriori* learning experience, in their editorial work, Murchland and his associates (1991) persuasively placed emphasis on civic education as the most effective mechanism for administering democratic governance in higher education. While they seem to have downplayed the power of civic intelligence, by and large, the role of civic intelligence is seen rather as embedded in the business and implicitly in the stated mission of higher education. Civic intelligence, according to Mathews (in Murchland, 1991), "means having the capacity to find out both what the facts are and what those facts mean to others….Is for sorting out whether our estimations of various options before us are consistent with those things we value in our common life" (pp. 51 & 53).

It seems, however, that they gave slightly more credence to the impact of civic education more than civic intelligence unless it is translated into civic action, which from their perspective is that for which civic education actually responsible. This may seem questionable to some since Socrates contended that the content of a subject that one teaches is a reflection of the individual's intelligence, and those who are teachable reflect the responsiveness of their own intelligence (Plato, 1981). It can thus be argued that the effectiveness of a civic education is associated with civic intelligence. In a way, this viewpoint seems to point to Murchland and his associates' assertion that civic intelligence must be translated into civic action. But then, one probably cannot induce any democratic action until the civic intelligence is stimulated through civic education to produce an ideal civic action. It is perhaps with these notions that Benjamin (1950) posited:

> The achievement of mutual support between the theory and the practice of educational democracy requires the discovery and utilization of certain formal, basic relationships among all those engaged in college and university work. The essence of all those relationships is *fairness*, the spirit by which men develop and use the instruments of democracy....With this spirit, the simplest and most direct measures of communication and action can be the soul of democracy. The letter of university democracy sometimes killeth when the spirit of fairness maketh not alive. *Theory* illumines purposes, practice achieves purposes, and *fairness* guards and develops those purposes for every individual. This is a clear-cut and simply stated program for the administration of higher education. (p. viii)

Table 2.3 summarizes the evaluation of the Breadth Theories' premise on democratic governance and the administration of higher education in civic society.

Table 2.3, Appraisal Summary of the Breadth Theories

Breadth Theories	*Theory of Democratic Governance*	*Tenet of Higher Education Administration*	*Metaphor of Democratic/ Civic Education*	*Public Policy on Open Access & Enrollment Management*
Benjamin and Associates	Democracy is an idyllic mode of association whereby a society orders its way of governance, and democratic education is a framework that helps shape this ideal.	The quality of higher education, civic culture, and social progress in democratic society is in accordance with the degree of national development.	Democratic process is *organic*, geared toward *security*, *productivity*, and *cultivation* management for higher culture development.	Access to higher education should not be based upon students' economic well-being, as such grants-in-aid should be freely provided so as to counteract the antidemocratic effects of money barriers to college admissibility.
Breneman and Finn	In the administration of democratic governance, public policy should be responsive to society's overall interests in the nature, scope, and purposes of higher education as it approaches a decade or more of limited growth or retrenchment.	The distinctive features of the free enterprise system, which distinguishes the public and private higher education sectors, tend to suggest that not every venture may be successful since the potential for failure is unpredictably associated with independence and innovation.	The equitability of service in federal student aid programs for both private and public higher education depends on the *fit* between the costs of attending particular colleges and the levels of assistance provided by those particular federal programs.	Due to the magnitude of the interplay of federal programs and enrollment demands in higher education, if student subsidies are not favored by equitable policy to open access, the trade-off between access and choice will continue to the extent that fewer students will be helped.

Dewey	A democracy is more than a form of government; it is primarily a mode of associated living, of conjoint communicated experience.	To achieve the democratic goal of education for both the individual and society, it must be based upon the quality of learning experience, and in understanding the process of invigorating the educational experiences, it must allow the citizens to fulfill their potential as members of society.	People associate for all sorts of purposes, which grow and take shape through the process of *social intelligence* that arises from the association of two principles— *continuity* and *interaction*.	The context of progressive education is to promote the freedom of social intelligence, since freedom resides in the operations of intelligent observation and judgment by which a purpose is developed; guidance given in exercising the intelligence is an aid to democratic freedom.
Pinkney	Democracy is not part of the natural order of life, but a cause rather than effect of reconciliation between groups. Interaction of the complex groups' interests and demands of the political makeup constitute conflicts in the political processes, which reflect the framework within which different political ideologies inform or catalyze political actions or persuasions in the context of democratic governance.	The configuration of varied interests and demands of social groups, such as higher education, religious institutions, and trade unions, including formal political structures of society, have the propensity to cause a transition to democracy. The universities, for instance, served as the most effective social institutions in Ghanaian politics for the campaign toward democracy.	The nature of democracy is *elusive* both as a concept and as a feasible objective. As a concept, democracy can be classified into six ideological tendencies: *radical, guided, liberal, socialist, consociational,* and *populist* democracies.	In the context of radical democratic governance, a retrenchment policy is likely to weaken at least three major power bases: 1) Beneficiaries of government patronage will suffer job losses. 2) Urban poor will suffer a reduction in social services, economic inflation. 3) The productive sector will depend more on market forces than on favorable government intervention.

Murchland and Associates	The politics of democratic governance in higher education administration is necessarily an education in the practice of making varieties of choices with others who are different from us, and the conflicts inevitable in such choices produce the necessary pressure that leads the citizenry to learn and to develop social intelligence toward civic responsibility.	Universities serve democracy as gatekeepers of valuable social offices, sanctuaries of non-repression, and as associational communities. Therefore, it must educate citizens for democratic society by: 1) Ensuring civic literacy in the principles on which democratic/political culture is based. 2) Providing civic education that teaches civic values and emphasizes civic skills for ideal democratic action and leadership. 3) Developing civic competence through commitment to social services and community projects.	Democratic governance in higher education can be associated with the metaphor of the *marketplace transactions* for which the civic society is perceived as the producers and consumers than as just mere citizens, since it shaped our self-understanding as a nation.	Higher education should give priority to the democratic principle of nondiscrimination over efficiency in their admissions procedures.

CONCLUSION

It is inconceivable that ideal democratic governance can be administered in the absence of the social institutions that educate the citizenry for democratic living. As most of the Breadth Theories persuasively argued, this educative tool is democratic education by which the social intelligence of the citizenry is stimulated toward civic responsibility. Though there is a great gap between the civic mission of the institutions of higher education and the reality of their commitments to those democratic ideals (Murchland, 1991), it is not a complacent civic goal displacement. Society and the system of governance cannot afford such complacency, for if they do, the social and cultural infrastructures will collapse to the detriment of the citizenry (Benjamin, 1950 & 1967). More so, the fabric of national development for which democratic governance is required also points to higher education's role as an educative liaison between the political culture and the culture of the populace (Benjamin, 1950 & 1967; McDonnell, Timpane, & Benjamin, 2000; & Murchland, 1991). That means higher education can be perceived as the *catalyst* that helps make the culture of politics and of the citizenry *learn* how to stick together in order to operationalize their collective purposes for the ideal democratic governance.

Since the learning itself is "a relatively permanent change in an organism's behavior due to experience" (Myers, 2002, p. 225), in its role as a *catalyst*, higher education can thus induce social change through democratic education. The context of this democratic education is what Dewey (1916 & 1938) contended as progressive education, a framework that takes into crucial account the personal learning experiences and freedom in exercising social intelligence of the individual toward social change. While some change can be progressive, instantaneous, or static, in Murchland (1991), Pitkin and Shumer posited that, "Democracy is our best means for achieving social change and remain our conscious goal" (p. 114). Congruent with a democratic goal pursuit is the need to fill a civic vacuum, which means the democracy for social change must address where the gap exists in the democratic governance of civic society. Addressing the concern of contemporary democratic governance and the role of higher education in this process, Flynn, Milliron, De Los Santos, and Miles (2003) persuasively assert: "We are not ready to prevent or respond to a swath of Homeland Security threats that appear all the more likely to materialize in the decade to come. Most leaders and policymakers recognize that a key to readiness is targeted education and training...focused on Homeland Security issues" (para. 2). So then, Mathews's suggestion that the "Academe lost interest in civic education centuries ago when thought was separated from action and the academic disciplines were born" (in Murchland, 1991, p. 49), is an indication of an inquiry toward social change.

REFERENCES

Ball, T., & Dagger, R. (2002). *Political ideologies and the democratic ideal* (4th ed.). New York: Addison Wesley.

Barber, B. R. (1991). The civic mission of the university. In B. Murchland (Ed.), *Higher education and the practice of democratic politics: A political education reader* (pp. 160-169). Dayton, OH: Kettering Foundation.

Baradat, L. P. (2003). *Political ideologies: Their origins and impact* (8th ed.). Upper Saddle River, NJ: Pearson Education.

Benjamin, H. R. W. (1950). *Democracy in the administration of higher education.* New York: Harper.

Benjamin, H. R. W. (1965). *Higher education in the American republics.* New York: McGraw-Hill.

Breneman, D. W., & Finn, Jr., C. E. (1978). *Public policy and private higher education.* Washington, D.C: The Brookings Institution.

Cohen, B. J., & Orbuch, T. L. (1990). *Introduction to sociology.* New York: McGraw-Hill.

Cook, C. E. (1998). *Lobbying for higher education: How colleges and universities influence federal policy* (1st ed.). Nashville, TN: Vanderbilt University Press.

Corwin, E. S. (1920). *The constitution and what it means to-day.* Princeton, NJ: Princeton University Press.

Democracy and governance: A conceptual Framework. (1998, November). Washington, D.C: Center for Democracy and Governance

Detention without trial: The Quarshigah "conspiracy." (1990, July). London, UK: Amnesty International News Release & Report.

Dewey, J. (1916). *Democracy and education: An introduction to the philosophy of education.* New York: Macmillan.

Dewey, J. (1997). *Democracy and education: An introduction to the philosophy of education.* New York: The Free Press.

Dewey, J. (1938). *Experience and education.* New York: Macmillan.

Ehrlich, T. (Ed.). (2000). *Civic responsibility and higher education* Phoenix: American Council on Education and Oryx Press.

Eyler, J., & Giles, D. E. (1999). *Where's the learning in service-learning.* San Francisco, CA: Jossey-Bass.

Etzioni, A. (1993). *The spirit of community: The reinvention of American society.* New York: Crown.

Fear of ill-treatment/legal concern. (1992, December). London, UK: Amnesty International News Release & Report.

Flynn, R. T., Milliron, M. D., De Los Santos, G. E., & Miles, C. L. (2003, July). Homeland Security and the Community College: A vibrant present and vital future [Abstract]. League for Innovation in the Community College: *Leadership Abstracts, 16, 7.*

Ghana: Political imprisonment used to silence government critics. (1991, December). London, UK: Amnesty International News Release & Report.

Government denies existence of political prisoners: Minister says detainees "safer" in custody. (1991, August). Washington, DC: Africa Watch.

Grigsby, E. (1999). *Analyzing politics: An introduction to political science.* New York: West/Wadsworth.

Groof, J. D., Neave, G., & Svec, J. (1998). *Democracy and governance in higher education.* Boston, Massachusetts: Kluwer Law International.

Gutmann, A. (1991). The primacy of political education. In B. Murchland (Ed.), *Higher education and the practice of democratic politics: A political education reader* (pp. 69-82). Dayton, OH: Kettering Foundation.

Hand, H. C. (1950). Studying the students and their communities. In H. Benjamin (Ed.), *Democracy in the administration of higher education* (pp. 77-92 & 165-179). New York: Harper.

Haskew, L. D. (1950). Securing and distributing financial support. In H. Benjamin (Ed.), *Democracy in the administration of higher education* (pp. 149-180). New York: Harper.

Held, D. (1987). *Models on democracy.* Stanford, California: Stanford University Press.

Higher Education for American Democracy: A Report of the President's Commission on Higher Education. (1947). (vols. 1-3). Washington, D.C: U.S. Government Printing Office.

Hickey, W. H.., Voorhees, C. V., & Associates (1969). *The role of the school in community education.* Midland, MI: Pendell.

Hornbake, R. L. (1950). Selecting and developing appropriate institutional activities. In H. Benjamin (Ed.), *Democracy in the administration of higher education* (pp. 181-203). New York: Harper.

Jacoby, B., & Associates (1996). *Service-learning in higher education: concepts and practices* (1st ed.). San Francisco, California: Jossey-Bass.

Kludze, A. K. P. (1993, May). *Ghana: Constitutional chronology.* In Blaustein, A. P., Editor, & Flanz, G. H., Editor (Eds.). *Constitutions of the countries of the world* (pp. v–xviii). New York: Oceana.

Lawyers detained for commemorating judges' murder: Human rights and the law under the PNDC government. (1989, July). Washington, DC: Africa Watch.

Library of Congress (2003, March 24). Ghana: A country study. *Federal Research Division.* Retrieved September 6, 2003, from http://lcweb2.loc. gov/frd/cs/ghtoc.html.

Maddox, W.S., & Lilie, S.A. (1984). *Beyond liberal and conservative: Reassessing the political spectrum.* New York: Cato Institute.

Mark, R. (1996). *Research made simple: A handbook for social workers.* Thousand Oaks, CA: SAGE.

Mathews, D. (1991). Civic intelligence. In B. Murchland (Ed.), *Higher education and the practice of democratic politics: A political education reader* (pp. 48-55). Dayton, OH: Kettering Foundation.

McDonnell, L. M., Timpane, P. M. & Benjamin, R. W. (Eds.). (2000). *Rediscovering the democratic purposes of education.* Lawrence, KS: University Press of Kansas.

McPherson, M. S. (1978). The demand for higher education. In D. W. Breneman & C. E. Finn, Jr. (Eds.). *Public policy and private higher education* (pp. 143-196). Washington, D.C: The Brookings Institution.

Murchland, B. (Ed.). (1991). *Higher education and the practice of democratic politics: A political education reader.* Dayton, OH: Kettering Foundation.

Myers, D. G. (2002). *Exploring psychology* (5th ed.). New York: Worth.

Neugeboren, B. (1991). *Organization, policy, and practice in the human services.* New York: The Haworth Press.

Official attacks on religious freedom. (1990, May). Washington, DC: Africa Watch.

O'Sullivan, E., Rassel, G. R., & Berner, M. (2003). *Research methods for public administrators* (4th ed.). New York: Longman.

Pinkney, R. (1997). *Democracy and dictatorship in Ghana and Tanzania.* London, Great Britain: MacMillan Press.

Pinkney, R. (1994). *Democracy in the Third World.* Boulder, Colorado: Lynne Rienner.

Plato, (1981). *Meno* (2nd ed.). Grube, G. M. A. (Trans.). Indianapolis, IN: Hackett.

Political imprisonment and the death penalty. (1991, December). London, UK: Amnesty International News Release & Report.

Putnam, R. D. (2000). *Bowling alone: The collapse and revival of American community.* New York: Touchstone Book.

Revolutionary injustice: Abuse of the legal system under the PNDC govern-ment. (1992, January). Washington, DC: Africa Watch.

Schapiro, S. A. (Ed.). (1999). *Higher education for democracy: Experiments in progressive pedagogy at Goddard College.* New York: Peter Lang.

Schramm, R. (1999). Extending democracy from classroom to school-house: Studying democratic governance at Goddard College. In S. A. Schapiro (Ed.), *Higher education for democracy: Experiments in progressive pedagogy at Goddard College* (pp. 249-273). New York: Peter Lang.

Shafritz, J. M., & Russell, E. W. (2000). *Introducing public administration* (2nd ed.). New York: Addison Wesley Longman.

Singleton, R. A., Jr., & & Straits, B. C. (1988). *Approaches to social research* (3rd ed.). New York: Oxford University Press.

Skocpol, T., & Fiorina, M. P. (Eds.). (1999). *Civic engagement in American democracy.* Washington, DC: Brookings Institute Press.

Taylor, H. (1950). The task of college administration. In H. Benjamin (Ed.), *Democracy in the administration of higher education* (pp. 25-47). New York: Harper.

The death penalty in Ghana. (1985, September). London, UK: Amnesty International News Release & Report.

The public tribunals in Ghana. (1984, July). London, UK: Amnesty International News Release & Report.

Triola, M. F. (2002). *Essentials of statistics.* Boston: Pearson/Addison-Wesley.

Walden University Catalog (2003-2004). Minneapolis, MN: Author.

Web-based Education Commission (2000). The power of the Internet for learning: Final report of Web-Based Education Commission. Retrieved May 23, 2003, from *http://www ed.gov/offices/AC/WBEC/ FinalReport/*Section1

Wilson, J. Q. (2000). *American Government: A brief version* (5th ed.). Boston, MA: Houghton Mifflin.

0-595-31465-1

Printed in the United States
92249LV00004B/502-558/A